The Intellectuals and the Flag

Todd Gitlin

The Intellectuals and the Flag

COLUMBIA UNIVERSITY PRESS

NEW YORK

COLUMBIA UNIVERSITY PRESS
Publishers Since 1893
New York   Chichester, West Sussex
Copyright © 2006 Todd Gitlin

Library of Congress Cataloging-in-Publication Data
Gitlin, Todd.
The intellectuals and the flag / Todd Gitlin
p. cm.
Includes bibliographical references and index.
ISBN 0–231–12492–9 (alk. paper) — ISBN 0–231–51035–7 (e-book)
1. United States—Intellectual life—20th century.
2. United States—Intellectual life—21st century.
3. Intellectuals—United States—Biography. 4. Civics.
5. Nationalism—United States. 6. Liberalism—United States.
7. Radicalism—United States. 8. Political culture—United States.
9. United States—Politics and government—1945–1989.
10. United States—Politics and government—1989–
I. Title

E169.12.G58   2005
973.92'086'31—dc22   2005049779

Columbia University Press books are printed
on permanent and durable acid-free paper.

Printed in the United States of America
c 10 9 8 7 6 5 4 3 2 1

To my students

Contents

The Intellectuals and the Flag

Introduction: From Great Refusal to Political Retreat

This book assumes that political thinking matters to the fate of American democracy and therefore to the prospect for decency in the world. It also has a more specific objective: to contribute to a new start for intellectual life on the left.

But surely this sounds presumptuous. Why should political intellectuals of the left need a new start? It is hard—perhaps impossible—to disentangle the practical from the philosophical reasons, for they are intertwined. All in all, the criticism of established arrangements—which is the left's specialty—does not convince a critical mass of the populace to put the critics in charge. Even if the critics are right to chastise the authorities as they see fit, many people do not see the critics as responsible, reliable, or competent to govern. They see them as another upper crust: a "new class" of "limousine liberals" and "cultural elitists." Those of the left's political-intellectual traditions that have flourished in recent decades, however worthy at times for moral self-definition, have led us into a wilderness. For all the intense emphasis in recent years on identity politics, political thought has purposes that reach far beyond self-definition. It has to make itself felt. It has to be useful.

This might, on the face of it, be a healthy time for an intellectual renaissance. The nation is deeply troubled, and for all the cant about optimism and faith, much of the nation *knows* it is troubled. Intellectuals in particular despair of public discourse—

reasonably so—and despair might prove, this time, to be the birth mother of invention. What resources, then, do Americans have for thinking freshly? Surprisingly few. The Marxism and postmodernism of the left are exhausted. Conservative thought has collapsed into market grandiosity and nationalist bombast. Surely, for more reasons than one, these are times that try men's souls—in terms that Tom Paine would have found sometimes familiar (the urgency, certainly) and sometimes strange. This nation (as well as others) is besieged by murderous enemies, yet beneath the repetition of stock phrases—"war on terror," "axis of evil," "root causes"—is precious little public discussion of how this state of affairs came to pass and what can be done about it. Rarely does a fair, thorough, intelligible public debate take place on any significant political subject. But that is not to say that the country is inert. To the contrary, the attentive populace is highly charged and intensely polarized. Eventually, even the ostrich side of the left had to recognize that since the mid-1970s it had been outfought by a disciplined alliance of plutocrats and right-wing fundamentalist Christians: that a political bloc equipped with big (if crude) ideas and ready for sledgehammer combat had seized the country's commanding heights. But many on the left do not recognize quite how they lost or understand how to recover.

During this period the hallmark of left-wing thought has been negation—*resistance* is the more glamorous word. Intellectuals of the left have been playing defense. It is as if history were a tank dispatched by the wrong army, and all that was left to do was to stand in its way and try to block it. If we had a manual, it would be called, *What Is Not to Be Done*. We are the critics—it is for others to imagine a desirable world and a way to achieve it. The left has gotten comfortable on the margins of political life, and for intellectuals it has been no different. The left speaks of "resistance" and "speaking truth to power." But resistance presupposes that power has the initiative—resistance is its negative pole.

"Speaking truth to power," an old Quaker ideal of virtuous conduct, is a more problematic approach than it appears at first blush, for it presupposes that the party of power is counterposed to the party of truth. In this scenario the intellectual is the torchbearer of opposition, invulnerable to the seductions of power—

indeed, the left posits that one can recognize the truth by being indifferent to power. That indifference verges on the definitional. Being powerful is proof that one has sold out.

So there is a purity to the will. There is also more than a little futility—what Herbert Marcuse in 1964 called the "Great Refusal," the absolute rejection of the social order.[1] At a time when the civil rights movement was on the brink of triumph and the New Left was ascendant, Marcuse was convinced that the United States exemplified a "one-dimensional" society, a state of intellectual impoverishment so all embracing as to have seeped into the seemingly inviolable identity of the person, body-snatched him so thoroughly as to have devoured his soul, and converted the denatured remnant into—in the title of Marcuse's once-influential book—a one-dimensional man. The Great Refusal plays to a hope of redemption in some glimmering future because it despairs of the present. Because the present is slammed shut, one finds solace in an imagined future—an act of faith that is, at the very least, naive, given the refuser's conviction that closure is fate. The Great Refusal is the triumph of German romanticism. (Even the initials are apt.) Inside the idea of the Great Refusal lives a despair that the left can—or, in truth, needs to—break out of the prison of its margins.

The Great Refusal is a shout from an ivory tower. It presupposes that the intellectuals live in a play with two characters: the speakers of truth and the powers. The play challenges the onlookers to declare themselves: which side are you on? But in the world of ordinary life, the overwhelming bulk of the populace belong to neither camp. Most people live in an apolitical world and rarely feel that they need to choose sides. Moral purity tends to leave them cold. Indeed, as most of them see it, the intellectuals are more alien than the powers, who at least can feign "speaking their language." Despite the growing percentage of Americans who graduate from college—between 1960 and 2003, the percentage of college graduates in the adult population almost quadrupled, from 7.7 to 27.2 percent of those aged twenty-five and older[2]—anti-intellectualism has not receded: far from it. The powers' demagogic techniques—their propagandistic smoothness, combined with the media's deference—match up well with popular credulity. So those who do not normally concern themselves with politics feel closer to the powers than to the intellectuals. It is to the powers—or to celebrities or to each other—that they turn when they feel fearful, embattled, needy. To them the intellectuals tend to look like a sideshow of sneering, self-serving noisemakers.

I do not speak as a stranger to the feeling when I say that the rapture of resistance bespeaks a not-so-quiet desperation. In the joyful ferocity of the reaction, is there not a bit of a prideful recognition that the critic has, with the best will in the world, painted himself or herself into a corner? Doesn't defeat taste sweet in a good cause? The honest truth is that negativity has its rewards and they are far from negligible. Self-satisfaction is a crisp and soothing satisfaction. It grants nobility. It stokes the psychic fires. Defeated outrage cannot really be defeated. It burns with a sublime and cleansing flame. It confirms one's righteousness. It collapses the indeterminate future into a burning present.

This pride in marginality bursts out in many forms—crude and sophisticated, rhetorical and scholarly, intellectual and tactical. In presidential politics we saw it in Ralph Nader's doomed and reckless runs for the White House, in his unmodulated fury at the Democratic Party for its corrupt bargains with corporate interests, in the satisfaction he exhibited at the triumph of George W. Bush in 2000, in his refusal—reminiscent of Bush's—to acknowledge any trace of error, any miscalculation of cause and effect, in the bright, straight, heedless line of his crusade for the right and the true. In street politics we have seen it in the sort of militancy that seeks confrontations with the police or Starbucks, measuring triumphs by the tactical panache of its confrontations and boasting of its indifference to the reactions of the misguided and uncool multitude. This is closer to the triumph of spectacle than the triumph of politics. It is the joy of subjectivity—the displacement of the goal from power (an objective fact) to empowerment (a subjective experience).

In this tradition—for a tradition it has become—power is the spook, as Arthur Miller put it in a fine, neglected essay about the 1960s and the New Left's rebellion against the Old.[3] Fundamentally, Miller understood, the New Left was an anarchist movement—revolted by power wherever it found it, whether in Soviet communism, overweening corporations, or brutal U.S.

force in Vietnam. It was an opposition—not simply to the existing government but to power *period*. Oppositional anarchism is especially congenial for *student* movements. As the sociologists Irving L. Horowitz and William H. Friedland observed, student activists of the sixties were primed to be anarchists, requiring little (if any) formal organization in order to flourish, because students were rather well educated to run meetings, divide labor, communicate with each other, and otherwise make things happen—an accurate observation, in my experience.[4] The rise of the Internet makes the anarchist spirit even more efficacious, for massive lobbies and fund-raising apparatuses (like MoveOn.org) and giant demonstrations (like that in Seattle at the World Trade Organization meetings in 1999 and in New York at the Republican Convention in 2004) can be cobbled together without need of a central office or much formal structure.

The New Left revolt against power was also a revolt against authority—sometimes, that is, against *legitimate* power. It wasn't only economic, political, and military power that the student movement resisted: it was the claim to knowledge, the bedrock of professionalism itself. Again and again in various settings the New Left—and, even more, the counterculture—asked, What is the standing of those who speak? Who needs them? Why listen to *these* journalists (corporate-fed creatures), *these* intellectuals (mouthpieces for vested interests), *these* doctors and lawyers and city planners (speaking for their own vested interests)—even *these* leaders of the student movement itself (or at least those whom the media anoint as their spokesmen)?[5] So, in a certain respect, the New Left was a self-undermining movement. Some of the later New Left's hero worship of revolutionary leaders and Marxist-Leninist movements abroad—or at home, in the domestic slice of the Third World—was, I believe, a displaced and distorted accommodation to authority on the part of a movement that was reluctant to acknowledge any authority of its own.

When the left-moving tide of the sixties had run out, minds moved on, and so did the search for realigned principles of authority. The New Left's graduates and successors pursued their quarrel with the universities in manifold ways. Historians promoted "history from the bottom up." Literature professors elevated the writings of the obscure. Philosophers of science punctured what they saw as the pretenses of objectivity. In effect, all were pursuing justifications for their own authority. Through their disciplinary choices and otherwise, the professionals who evolved from the student movement were playing out its core ambivalence toward authority—on the one hand, deeply doubting the legitimacy of experts, on the other, becoming experts themselves. How would ambitious young intellectuals manage this delicate task?

One answer was "theory"—the welter of poststructuralist, literary-critical, psychoanalytic, neo-Marxist, feminist, queer, and related writings that gathered prestige in the humanities and social sciences in the 1970s, thanks to their European (usually French) lineage, the glee and often breathtaking ingenuity with which the concepts were tossed around, and the blithe freedom from draggy old empirical proof. Another answer was categorical opposition to U.S. foreign policy—a hostility that, however justified in particular instances, spilled out so unreservedly as to negate any possibility of a reformed America that would be worth fighting for. But neither "theory" nor the big anti-imperialist No could engage real political dynamics or possibilities. Both were, in the end, metaphysical.

This book consists of essays that I have written since 1988 and rewritten for this occasion to clarify their thrust. They add up to an argument that intellectual life on the American left must recover from its main drift and transcend its accommodation to political defeat. At a time when radical intellectuals imagine themselves floating free of national connection, fearful that *national* automatically means *nationalist* and *practical* means *corrupt*, liberal and radical intellectuals—those who deeply value liberty and equality—should commit ourselves to political recovery and a regeneration of American possibilities. In a previous book, *Letters to a Young Activist* (2003), I defended practical efforts at politics toward that end. *The Intellectuals and the Flag* aims to contribute to the work of putting an intellectual foundation under such efforts.

This book is divided into three parts. The first reviews the work of three exemplary intellectuals of past decades—mentors of mine (David Riesman and Irving Howe in the flesh, C. Wright Mills on the page)—and honors the scope of their work while exploring their limits. The second reviews the situation of left-wing intellectuals in our institutions of higher learning, asking why Riesman, Mills, and Howe have gone without clear successors. The third aims to resurrect a liberal ideal of patriotism in the awful aftermath of September 11, 2001, refusing to bow to the notion that the proper reply to mass murder is plutocracy, zealotry, and indiscriminate war.

Notes

1. Herbert Marcuse, *One-Dimensional Man* (Boston: Beacon, 1964), p. 63.
2. U.S. Census Bureau, *Statistical Abstract of the United States, 2003* (Washington, D.C.: U.S. Department of Commerce, 2004), no. 212.
3. Arthur Miller, introduction to Ken Kesey, *Kesey's Garage Sale* (New York: Viking, 1973), p. xv.
4. Irving L. Horowitz and William H. Friedland, *The Knowledge Factory: Student Power and Academic Politics in America* (Chicago: Aldine, 1971), p. 10.
5. On dilemmas of leadership in the New Left under the media spotlight, see Todd Gitlin, *The Whole World Is Watching* (Berkeley: University of California Press, 1980), chap. 5.

I. Three Exemplary Intellectuals

Intellectuals of the left need to do more than dissent—or praise. We need to see the world steadily and see it whole: to see without blinkers, to explain how things came to be as they are, to sharpen values and make them explicit, to sketch visions, to connect with publics in such a way as to suggest where our limping democracy might go. All this is our calling, even—or especially—in a time when most of the people one would expect to be paying attention, the morally alert young, are otherwise occupied.

"Ideology is a brain disease," said Jerry Rubin in the late 1960s, when he was riding high as a media-fueled, drug-fueled, shoot-from-the-lip Yippie celebrity, and virtually everyone in the United States outside the right wing would today agree. So-called movement conservatives harbor grand ideas of robust entrepreneurship that thrives on the outskirts of shriveled government—"the ownership society" is their phrase—while they selectively rely upon robust government to enforce moralist discipline. These, at least, are big ideas, if contradictory ones. But outside the right's ranks, big ideas and methodical thinking are out, specifics and practicality are in. The end of ideology (meaning the end of left-wing ideology) prematurely heralded by Daniel Bell in 1960 did eventually arrive, leaving the few activists of the left who aspire to sweeping change either sentimental about one or another variant of the Marxist iconography or stranded without even nostalgia to fall back on. When I see young people of a leftish bent fumble for a big picture of America in the world, they seem both earnest and marooned, and then once again I am dismayed at the left's (and not just the left's) intellectual default, all the more wrenching when we contrast it with the ambitions of the foremost intellectuals of the decades of my youth. Part I of this book is a tribute to three of the steadiest—their scope, their humanity, the intelligence of their efforts to make sense of a whole America.

True, the few young activists who do long for coherence may be starry-eyed about what ideology can accomplish and in their eagerness may not sufficiently appreciate the benefits of being liberated from the dark side of coherence. For a century, after all, there has been no more murderous force in the world than totalist ideologies. When Marxist-Leninists performed their parody of intellectual confidence, they wagered that the gods of consistency wouldn't mind their sacrifice of intellectual integrity. (Today's Islamists demand the same sort of sacrifice and offer other styles of devoted self-immolation.) The Leninists, Stalinists, Maoists, and Khmer Rouge enthusiasts need not disrupt their thought patterns to take account of inconvenient facts. Whatever happens, they always have an answer—because it is the same answer. (In the words of an old joke, when a Communist found out about Stalin's gulag, he was ready with a rejoinder: it was necessary, it didn't happen, and they're not doing it anymore.)

In fact, the few who long for ideology may actually be pining for something different: for a cogent morality, or a steady application of will, in other words, for stamina. Fighting desolation, bewilderment, and other forms of entropy, they resort to a parody of Enlightenment faith—a fusion of Enlightenment and religious fanaticism. Uncomfortable in the world as it is—and who possessed of a brain ought not to feel uncomfortable, given the last hundred years?—they devise a grid more to their liking, a world in which only the rational is real, as Hegel liked, but the rational is what the sacred texts decree to be rational, so that once the pattern of the future is clear, only a dose of ferocious will must be injected to tie up the world's loose ends. What they call ideology, in other words, is a sensibility—the sort of mind-melting, fevered tunnel vision that Dostoyevsky brilliantly described with awe and horror. It would seem like the triumph of intellect to conjure a mental scheme so comprehensive as to provide an exit from every conundrum. But in the end what the totalists have in mind is intellectual suicide.

When I began this book, or what turned out to be this book, before September 11, 2001, I had in mind a series of tributes to a number of American intellectuals who had influenced me in my youth. I was working on the third of these essays when the jetliners smashed into the World Trade Center. For a while my book was derailed. We had been slammed into a new era and I felt that bygone intellectuals of the left were largely useless, for they had been asking the wrong questions, offering little in the effort to come to grips with apocalyptic suicidal-homicidal Islamist fanatics. Of course it was not strictly the intellectuals' fault that the old systems of thought failed as prophecies: the explosive events had not yet occurred to discredit traditions, and it would be absurd to blame them for having failed to do Nostradamus duty. Yet this would not be the first time that Marxism, liberalism, and the other modern traditions had reported for intellectual duty empty handed. As Ira Katznelson argues in his stimulating book *Desolation and Enlightenment: Political Knowledge After Total War, Totalitarianism, and the Holocaust,*[1] the main traditions in political theory were also mute on the awful twentieth-century experiences of total violence. And as Susan Neiman maintains in her splendid *Evil in Modern Thought: An Alternative History of Philosophy*, the history of modern philosophy also needed to be rethought: while epistemology—the question of how we know what we know—has become philosophy's central subject, a deeper concern has been submerged, namely, the problem of evil that has haunted the main line of intellectual tradition since the seventeenth century.[2] Violence and evil: these are huge lapses, not minor omissions. It was as if a theory of air flight failed to leave room for the possibility that a plane whose engines slowed below a certain speed would lose lift and crash.

What do you say when bankruptcies of thought keep recurring? You conclude that you are dealing with a case of chronic impecuniousness. So the aftermath of the terror attacks was a fitting time to ask what we should now understand about the flaws—fundamental flaws—in our inherited intellectual systems. For several months I felt that we had been plunged into an emergency and that it was not solely a problem of security but an intellectual emergency as well. One piece of prime work to be done was an act—or, rather, two—of sweeping away. The foreign policy of George W. Bush was a multiple disaster—its own apocalyptic threat. ("Either you're with us or you're with the terrorists," a line he repeated scores of times.) But meanwhile the fundamentalist left stood in the way of what Michael Walzer, my former teacher and now colleague at *Dissent* magazine, called "a decent left." So I had a twin set of polemics to write and a lot of rethinking to do—and I am not finished with either.

In the process I came to recognize that most of the intellectuals I had set out to write about in the first place, generalists who had done their strongest work in the fifties and sixties, still mattered, and so did their conundrums and tensions. For one thing, their scope remained an inspiration. Of course, the breadth and lucidity of these intellectuals were part of what never ceased to impress me. But they weren't dilettantes. Without sacrificing scope they paid close attention to the fine grain of their subjects. Without confining themselves to minutiae, in the manner criticized by C. Wright Mills as "abstracted empiricism," they kept their feet on the ground even as they looked to the larger movements of history. With a largeness of vision now largely abandoned by social scientists and literary historians alike—among the rare contemporary exceptions are Walzer, the political theorist, and the political sociologist Michael Mann—they aspired to a coherent vision of the world as it was (and might be).

It wasn't just that David Riesman, C. Wright Mills, and Irving Howe wrote accessibly, even stylishly—this was certainly an attraction, but their lucidity by itself would not have commended them as exemplary. Nor was it just that they were, in their distinct ways, committed to changing the United States. They were activists, to be sure. But they were activists with a difference: activists who, in much different styles, and disagreeing, sometimes vigorously, about American predicaments, aspired to a coherence that would also, at the same time, make room for something new under the sun—or, if not altogether new, new in its weight and effect on the hitherto known world. Usually, without succumbing to received formulas they liked "taking it big," to use the phrase Mills used with his students, yet remained alert to the danger of grandiosity. Two sociologists and a literary critic, they extended themselves, whatever their work's ostensible subject, beyond it.

In the term made famous by Russell Jacoby before overuse made it banal, they were public intellectuals.[3] Note: *public* doesn't mean *freelance*. All three taught at universities (though Mills, toward the end of his life, thought he wanted to leave: Columbia would not permit him to teach a course on Marxism, and he was impatient with students). Their teaching positions were, whatever their besetting sins, more than convenient day jobs: they were, rather, hospitable platforms for free-ranging careers where a serious writer did not have to worry about how to please commercially minded publishers. The notion that writers for profitable magazines are somehow free of institutional commitments cheerfully overlooks all the ways in which the market functions as an institution (complete with gates and pressures), although its brick and mortar is harder to locate than a campus.

Mainly, Riesman, Mills, and Howe wanted to make the world more comprehensible to readers who were not professional intellectuals. The three free-ranging writers published in large-circulation general magazines as well as tiny ones, and their books made best-seller lists. In their time substantial figures like Hannah Arendt and James Baldwin wrote the higher journalism for the *New Yorker*. But none of them were, in Michael Bérubé's aptly wicked phrase, "publicity intellectuals," scattershot pundits promiscuous in their momentary appearances in the electronic media.[4] Even had they been invited more frequently, they probably would not have played. (Riesman considered television a debased forum and would not appear at all. Mills, on the other hand, suffered a major heart attack while cramming feverishly for a television debate.) They liked having audiences but refused to offer up caricatures of themselves. They believed in sustained argument, not punditry. No accident, since they cared about the whole of society and culture, they sometimes argued with each other. Each doubtful, in his own way, that intellectuals were entitled to rule, they did not veer over to self-loathing and take walks on the sound-bitten side. They would write clearly because making an effort to explain themselves was not only a public duty but a help to their own thinking. And they thought that thinking clearly was, in fair times or foul, a worthy enterprise for its own sake.

Notes

1. Katznelson, *Desolation and Enlightenment: Political Knowledge After Total War, Totalitarianism, and the Holocaust* (New York: Columbia University Press, 2003).
2. Neiman, *Evil in Modern Thought: An Alternative History of Philosophy* (Princeton, N.J.: Princeton University Press, 2002).
3. Jacoby, *The Last Intellectuals: American Culture in the Age of Academe* (New York: Basic Books, 1987).
4. Michael Bérubé, "Going Public," *Washington Post Book World,* July 7, 2002, p. BW03.

1
David Riesman's Lonely Crowd

In an age that views books as quaint artifacts on the fringes of the entertainment business, we may find it hard to recall that books ever guided national conversations in the United States. Sometimes the effect on history has been direct. Upton Sinclair's 1906 polemical novel, *The Jungle*, galvanized public sentiment in behalf of the Pure Food and Drug Act. In the 1960s Rachel Carson's *Silent Spring*, Michael Harrington's *The Other America*, Betty Friedan's *The Feminine Mystique*, and Ralph Nader's *Unsafe at Any Speed* helped the antipoverty, environmentalist, feminist, and consumer movements get under way, and subsequent re-form-minded conservative books, notably George L. Kelling and James Q. Wilson's *Fixing Broken Windows*, have had an equivalent effect.

But practical essays in advocacy are not the only books that count in public life. Sometimes books have mattered not by provoking action but by recognizing patterns, offering big interpretations of life, providing names for what, until the volumes appeared, were nothing more than hunches or diffuse sentiments. A serious book comes out, crystallizes a fear, a knack, or a hope into a big idea, a sweeping interpretation of reality that strikes a collective nerve in a large general public.[1] As in the case of Friedrich Hayek's *Road to Serfdom* (1944), Milton Friedman's *Capitalism and Freedom* (1962), and Charles A. Murray's *Losing Ground* (1984), a book may become a spur to a major ideological turn. In the case of Marshall

McLuhan's *Understanding Media* (1964), a book can furnish the media themselves with a vocabulary of self-recognition. Rarest of all is the book that penetrates popular consciousness so deeply that its insights become clichés, its wisdom conventional—to borrow a phrase devised, in fact, in one such book, *The Affluent Society* (1958), by John Kenneth Galbraith.

More than half a century ago Yale University Press published the first edition of *The Lonely Crowd,* by David Riesman, with Nathan Glazer and Reuel Denney, a book that contributed its own conceptual phrases to the American vocabulary.[2] The book's subject was nothing less than a sea change in American character: as the United States was moving from a society governed by the imperative of production to a society governed by the imperative of consumption, the character of its upper middle classes was shifting from "inner-directed" people, who as children internalized goals that were essentially "implanted" by elders, to "other-directed" people, "sensitized to the expectations and preferences of others."[3] In Riesman's metaphor the shift was from a life guided by an internal gyroscope to a life guided by radar. The new American no longer cared much about adult authority but rather was hyperalert to peer groups and gripped by mass media. Father might be reputed to know best, but if he did, it was increasingly because a television program said so.

The Lonely Crowd went on to become, according to a 1997 study by Herbert J. Gans, the best-selling book by a sociologist in U.S. history, with 1.4 million copies sold, largely in paperback editions.[4] (The first abridged edition, a pocket-size paperback, was one of the first beneficiaries of the wave of mass-market paperback editions.) For years the book made *inner-direction* and *other-direction* household terms, canapés for cocktail party chat. It was read by student radicals in the making, who overinterpreted its embrace of the search for autonomy as a roundhouse assault on conformity, when in fact Riesman was at pains to point out that any society ensures "some degree of conformity from the individuals who make it up," the question being how it secures that unavoidable conformity.[5] In the 1960s *The Lonely Crowd* was read as a harbinger of alienation leading to affluent revolt. Its title phrase even cropped up in a Bob Dylan song of 1967, "I

Shall Be Released." By the time he wrote his introduction to the 1969 edition, a more conservative Riesman was regretting that *"The Lonely Crowd* had contributed to the snobbish deprecation of business careers."[6]

The hoopla, the public embrace, not to mention misinterpretation, were all a far cry from original expectations. On publication in 1950 the book was greeted with respectful but frequently critical reviews in professional journals. When it came out in a paperback abridgment three years later, Riesman and Yale University Press expected the book to sell "a few thousand copies as a reading in social science courses."[7] Instead, it caught on. Why? With unerring hindsight we can see that it sympathetically exposed the anxieties of a middle class that was rising with the postwar boom, suburbanizing, busily availing itself of upgraded homes, machines, and status, relieved to be done with the depression and the war but baffled by cultural and psychological upheavals beneath the surface of everyday life.

Not least, *The Lonely Crowd* was jargon free (while inadvertently contributing its own either-or, quiz show style to the vocabulary of a culture that relishes bipolar categories, as with introvert/extrovert, hip/square, marginal/central). Today, sociological writing has all the public appeal of molecular biology, having substantially earned its reputation as a specialty for number crunchers and other pseudoscientific poseurs. By immense contrast, *The Lonely Crowd* was lucidly written, with a knack for puckish phrases: "inside-dopester," "the whip of the word," "from invisible hand to glad hand," "from the bank account to the expense account," "ambulatory patients in the ward of modern culture," "the friendship market," "wildcatting on the sex frontier," "the featherbed of plenty," "each life is an emergency." It was decidedly unpretentious, unforbidding in tone, omnicurious, with a feeling for recognizable types. Although demanding of the serious reader, and scarcely written in sound bites, it had the sound of an agreeable human voice, by turns chatty and approachably awkward, graceful and warm, nuanced and colloquial, sober and avuncular but frequently casual and good humored. Unlike most academic treatises, it did not get bogged down in definitional chatter. It was the book of a sympathetic citizen who wanted to counsel society, not lecture it.[8] It spoke directly to the people—Americans, largely, but not exclusively—whom it concerned (in both senses). It commiserated as it chastised, and even when it did chastise, it reassured the reader that one was not so lonely in one's anxieties as one might have imagined. It could be read with the reassurance of recognition. The style of speaking *to* rather than *about* has, since the mid-1950s, devolved into the self-help style, at the cost of intellectual seriousness, but *The Lonely Crowd* is proof that intelligent analysis can be directed to intelligent readers without treating them strictly as egocentric self-improvers.

Accessibility was not altogether unique in sociology in those years. In the 1950s even the professional journals were written so that any decently educated person could read them; books by C. Wright Mills made the best-seller lists, too. A large readership was willing to read something demanding that sensitively explored its condition and meditated on its costs. The popularity of *The Lonely Crowd* must also have owed something to the supple way that it ranged far and wide for its evidence, trotting through novels, children's books, movies, and anthropology. Although Riesman and Nathan Glazer were conducting formal interviews at the same time,[9] Riesman emphasized that he drew on them only slightly, that *The Lonely Crowd* was "based on our experiences of living in America—the people we have met, the jobs we have held, the books we have read, the movies we have seen, and the landscape."[10]

Though he was writing when television was still a new medium, Riesman took seriously the fact that Americans had been plunged into a media bath. He did so with concern but also without scorn. Even as television was still taking shape, he understood that the mass media were powerful in both content and form, and yet he did not succumb to the hype that characteristically greets each wave of technological marvels in American history.[11] He did not suppose that television would be able to rewrite the national character from scratch. As he put it, "Americans were ready for the mass media even before the mass media were ready for them."[12] A careful rereading of *The Lonely Crowd* shows, in fact, how sympathetic it is to mass media virtues—mainly, to television's challenging of provincialism and its cultivation of hybrid taste. With a sophisticated grasp of the cultural production process, *The Lonely Crowd* understood that the major reason for these benefits was that the media were headquartered in large metropolitan centers "where the pressures toward other-directed tolerance are greatest."[13] (This would remain the case even as the giant media corporations later spun off specialized channels for demographic niches.) In fact, although *The Lonely Crowd* was frequently read as an assault on other-direction, Riesman bent over backward to find virtue in the "considerateness, sensitivity and tolerance" characteristic of a society no longer gazing upward, toward elders and traditional authorities, for guidance.[14]

Interestingly, *The Lonely Crowd* survived the early collapse of one of its central hypotheses. This was the idea that each phase of social character (traditional, inner-directed, other-directed) corresponds to a rate of population growth. In her review of *The Lonely Crowd* in the *American Journal of Sociology*, Margaret Mead early observed that Riesman's evidence for the population theory was weak. She was not the only skeptic on this front. Riesman himself was aware in 1949, when the book was still in proofs, that the population model was seriously contested.[15] By the time of the book's 1969 reissue, Riesman had already renounced his demographic model. The revision didn't—and doesn't—matter. The book is so rich in observation that divergent readers will attend to different passages and feel themselves instructed. Mead herself pointed to a passage noting that other-directed conformism has predisposed Americans to project power centers outside the self—a reason that the paranoid streak in American life loomed so large and perhaps also a reason Americans were excessively afraid that the Russians would take them over. Myself, I have been struck by the prophetic quality of Riesman's discussion of the "inside-dopester" as a social type, whose goal is "never to be taken in by any person, cause or event."[16] Sam Donaldson, Cokie Roberts, Chris Matthews, and Company were imagined long before smirking became the lucrative style for Washington pundits. In sum, as Margaret Mead put it, "Almost every paragraph in this book incites one to theoretical speculation and . . . suggests to the reader additional lifetime programs of research."[17]

Inevitably, the book reads differently than it did half a century ago—although just as incisively. The starkness of the transition from inner-direction to other-direction was more evident to readers of the 1950s, caught up as they were in a sudden tide of affluence. Today, the book may not resonate in the same way. In the mid-1980s, while teaching *The Lonely Crowd* to freshmen and sophomores at Berkeley, I discovered that they had trouble grasping the key distinction between inner- and other-direction. Intuitively, it made little sense to them. This was not because, as Riesman had suggested, "the shift from inner-direction to other-direction [seems] unimportant by comparison with" the momentous shift from tradition-directed life to *both* inner- *and* other-direction—because, in other words, the shift from traditional society to the whole of modernity is *the* momentous transition in human history.[18] No, the distinction between inner- and other- was lost on students born after 1960, born into a world of rock music, television, and video games, because these students had lived their entire lives as other-directed, with radars. They took other-direction for granted. By the 1980s the "exceptional sensitivity to the actions and wishes of others" that Riesman held to be typical of other-direction had long since been institutionalized into the norms of talk shows and "sensitivity training."[19] The very category of "inner-direction" fell outside their experience. A life equipped with a psychic gyroscope had become well-nigh unimaginable.

Still, the open reader returns to *The Lonely Crowd* feeling many aftershocks of recognition. After the turn of the twenty-first century, the alert observer is made aware every day that the shift that Riesman discerned in the educated upper-middle classes of metropolitan centers has swept the country. In recent elections presidential candidates have been expected to answer the questions of ordinary men and women (Bill Clinton ingratiatingly, George H. W. Bush less so) and chat with reporters on camera during long bus trips (John McCain, Howard Dean, John Edwards). The remote, Wizard-of-Oz-like presidential aura belongs to a vanished yesteryear, along with a White House like Lincoln's, open for casual presidential chats.

Popular culture itself registers the sea change. Consider the differences between the quiz shows of the 1950s, *The $64,000 Question* and *Twenty-One,* and the hit series of 2000, *Who Wants to Be a Millionaire?* On *Twenty-One* the contestants were sealed off from influence in "isolation booths," with no hints, no multiple-choice questions; they were literally "inner-directed." On *Millionaire* in 2000 they stood out in the open, were given four prefab options from which to choose, and got to throw out "lifelines" to family, friends, and audience members. On the earlier shows questions concerned areas of special expertise like opera, boxing, and European royalty. Paul Farhi, an enterprising reporter for the *Washington Post*, put the difference this way:

On "The $64,000 Question" (1955–58) . . . a contestant was shown six portraits and asked to name not just the artist and the subject, but also the teacher with whom the artist had studied. Another contestant was asked to name the Verdi opera that started Arturo Toscanini's conducting career, as well as the date of the performance and its location. In 1957, a young college professor named Charles Van Doren was asked on "Twenty-One" to name the kings of Denmark, Norway, Sweden and Jordan. Herbert M. Stempel, the contestant who faced Van Doren and eventually exposed the rigging on "Twenty-One," was eliminated from the show when he could answer only two parts of the following three-parter: What was the name of the anti-populist Kansas newspaper editor of the 1920s? (William Allen White.) What was the name of his newspaper? (The Emporia Gazette.) What was the name of the column he wrote? ("What's the Matter With Kansas?")[20]

On *Millionaire,* by contrast, contestants could win huge sums by knowing "what two colors make up an Oreo cookie" or decide to pass up the chance to win by $500,000 by not taking a chance with, "How many von Trapp children were there in *The Sound of Music?*" In other words, the authority of knowledge derives largely from popular culture, knowledge shared with one's peers, not knowledge derived from the idiosyncrasies of personal mastery.

Granted, television today is far more widespread than in the late 1950s, so the educational level of viewers today is, on average, lower than before. But this factor by itself cannot explain the extent of the shift. It is likely that not only the knowledge base but the cultural aspirations of most Americans have changed.

No longer do Americans take pleasure in being stumped (except about the trivia of *popular* culture). Running into the limits of their knowledge would suggest (in gyroscopic fashion) that there is more to learn in the course of their lives. Today, in the name of "self-esteem" they are "sensitive" to their own weaknesses; they need to demonstrate how much they already know. "I am somebody" replaces "I will someday be somebody."

One longs for appropriately ambitious, germane studies of today's mentalities—books with the reach and approachability of *The Lonely Crowd* and its partial successor, *Habits of the Heart* (1985), by Robert Bellah and colleagues.[21] One wonders, in particular, how the concurrence of boom and growing inequality (and attendant anxieties) is playing in the consciousness of Americans, those who have benefited greatly as well as those who have benefited little or not at all. Sociology ought to be news that stays news, but few sociologists today extend their imaginations beyond narrow milieus to the biggest questions of social structure, culture and conflict. Their elders, hell-bent on professionalization, do not encourage range. It is worth noting that, like another of our outstanding sociologists, Daniel Bell, Riesman never was trained into writing a doctoral dissertation. He earned a law degree, clerked for Justice Louis Brandeis, and taught law school before relaunching his intellectual life.[22]

If I may close on a personal note: I met David Riesman during my sophomore year, in 1960, when he was a faculty adviser to the Harvard-Radcliffe peace group, Tocsin. A long-time critic of nationalism, Riesman had become deeply involved in writing and speaking against reliance on nuclear weapons, and I was amazed to learn that he, one of the most famous professors in the United States, was lending his station wagon to transport groups of peace activists to Vermont, to campaign for a pacifist member of Congress. Practicing the attitude that he commended, harboring both utopian hopes and practical ideas, Riesman always had time to chat about U.S. politics and society. He helped us raise money, contacted luminaries in our behalf, brought us to conferences, wrote follow-up letters after conversations. In fact, he famously wrote letters around the year and around the clock, sometimes more than one a day (he might have been the most prolific letter writer since

Thomas Jefferson), and while it was decidedly flattering for an undergraduate to be on the receiving end of such attention, Riesman did not take his mentoring lightly—that is, he was not afraid to disagree with us, sometimes vehemently, about some of our decisions. In those years he was also editing a journal of political commentary, the *Committee* (later *Council*) *of Correspondence Newsletter*. For decades he was, in fact, a one-man committee of correspondence. He was interested in everything. He picked up tiny references and gave back paragraphs of rumination and reference. The world is far-flung with hundreds of his correspondents, men and women of several generations who over the decades had the daunting experience of writing him a letter or sending him an article, only to receive back, often within a week, a much longer letter, two or three pages' worth at times, perhaps apologizing for a delay.

In his later years he became grumpy about many democratic changes in American life. His Tocquevillian fear of the "soft despotism" of the majority became more pronounced. His suspicion of authorities receded. His love of precision and detail led him toward an accommodation with mainstream sociology as it grew narrower, more quantitative and technical. Even so, he kept his distance from the doctrinal neoconservatism that attracted many generalist social scientists of his generation. (He told me once that curiosity had drawn him to travel in the Soviet Union in the thirties, but he was never a Marxist and had never flirted with communism or Trotskyism. Therefore he felt no need to invert his youthful commitments.) Well into his eighties he remained a stimulating, omnicurious observer and critic.

Max Weber, the century's greatest sociologist, famously deplored "specialists without spirit." Riesman, who was ninety-two when he died in 2002, gave of both mind and spirit without specialization. He deserves to be reread and his model honored.

Notes

1. Shallow books may strike comparable chords in the media, too, but they are more likely to be bought today, shelved tomorrow, and unread forevermore (though frequently alluded to).

2. If the question of authorship—that is, both credit and responsibility—should arise, partly because various editions of *The Lonely Crowd* appeared with varying credit lines, it should be noted that there is no dispute among the author and his collaborators. As Nathan Glazer has put the matter, *The Lonely Crowd* is "David Riesman's book. He conceived it, wrote most of it, and rewrote it for the final version. Contributions from the two listed co-authors in the form of initial drafts and research reports and rewritings of Riesman's first drafts may have spurred him to expand, revise, and extend his own thinking, but in the end it is his book" (Glazer, "Tocqueville and Riesman: Two Passages to Sociology," David Riesman Lecture on American Society, October 20, 1999, Department of Sociology, Harvard University, Cambridge, Mass., p. 1). It would seem that the frequent citation of Glazer and Denney as coauthors without Riesman's complaint is another instance of his generosity. Nonetheless, in introducing the book, I have kept to the original listing of the authors.

3. David Riesman, with Nathan Glazer and Reuel Denney, *The Lonely Crowd* (1950; reprint, New Haven, Conn.: Yale University Press, 1969), p. 8.

4. Herbert J. Gans, "Best Sellers by American Sociologists: An Exploratory Study," in Dan Clawson, ed., *Required Reading: Sociology's Most Influential Books* (Amherst: University of Massachusetts Press, 1998), pp. 19–27.

5. Riesman, Glazer, and Denney, *The Lonely Crowd*, p. 5.

6. Riesman, introduction to *The Lonely Crowd*, p. xviii.

7. Ibid., p. xli.

8. I borrow some phrases here from my "Sociology for Whom? Criticism for Whom?" in Herbert J. Gans, ed., *Sociology in America* (Newbury Park, Calif.: Sage, 1990), p. 221.

9. Later published in David Riesman with Nathan Glazer, *Faces in the Crowd* (New Haven, Conn.: Yale University Press, 1952).

10. Riesman, introduction to *The Lonely Crowd*, p. lxi.

11. His few sentences on the impact of print and its profusion (pp. 89, 96) are a concise marvel anticipating some of Marshall McLuhan's stronger ideas.

12. Riesman, introduction to *The Lonely Crowd*, p. liii.

13. Riesman, Glazer, and Denney, *The Lonely Crowd*, p. 192.

14. Riesman, introduction to *The Lonely Crowd*, p. xxxii.

15. Ibid., p. xlii.

16. Riesman, Glazer, and Denney, *The Lonely Crowd*, p. 182.

17. Margaret Mead, *American Journal of Sociology* 61 (1951): 496—97.

18. Riesman, Glazer, and Denney, *The Lonely Crowd*, p. 13.

19. Ibid., p. 22.

20. Paul Farhi, "Ask a Stupid Question and Millions of People Will Tune Right In," *Washington Post*, January 6, 2000, p. C1.

21. *Habits of the Heart: Individualism and Commitment in American Life* (New York: Harper and Row, 1986).

22. Bell received a doctoral degree from Columbia for his published book, *The End of Ideology: On the Exhaustion of Political Ideas in the Fifties* (Glencoe, Ill.: Free Press, 1960).

2

C. Wright Mills, Free Radical

1

Whether the rest of this sentence sounds like an oxymoron or not, C. Wright Mills was the most inspiring sociologist of the second half of the twentieth century, his achievement all the more remarkable given that he died at forty-five and produced his major work in a span of little more than a decade. For the political generation trying to find its bearings in the early sixties, Mills was a guiding knight of radicalism. Yet he was a bundle of paradoxes, and this was part of his appeal, whether his readers were consciously attuned to the paradoxes or not.

He was a radical disabused of radical traditions, a sociologist disgruntled with the course of sociology, an intellectual frequently skeptical of intellectuals, a defender of popular action as well as a craftsman, a despairing optimist, a vigorous pessimist, and, all in all, one of the few contemporaries whose intelligence, verve, passion, scope—and contradictions—seemed alert to most of the main moral and political traps of his time. A philosophically trained and best-selling sociologist who decided to write pamphlets, a populist who scrambled to find what was salvageable within the Marxist tradition, a loner committed to politics, a man of substance acutely cognizant of style, he was not only a guide but an exemplar, prefiguring in his paradoxes some of the tensions of a student movement that was reared on privilege amid exhausted ideologies yet hell-bent on finding, or forging, a way to transform the United States root and branch.[1]

In his two final years Mills the writer became a public figure, his tracts against the Cold War and U.S. Latin American policy more widely read than any other radical's, his *Listen, Yankee,* featured on the cover of *Harper's Magazine,* his "Letter to the New Left" published in both the British *New Left Review* and the American *Studies on the Left* and distributed, in mimeographed form, by Students for a Democratic Society. In December 1960, while cramming for a television debate on Latin America policy with an established foreign policy analyst, Mills suffered a heart attack, and when he died fifteen months later he was instantly celebrated as a martyr.[2] SDS's Port Huron Statement carries echoes of Mills's prose, and Tom Hayden, its principal author, wrote his master's thesis on Mills, whom he labeled "Radical Nomad," a heroic if quixotic figure who, like the New Left itself, tried to muscle a way through the ideological logjam. After Mills's death at least one son of founding New Left parents was named for him, along with at least one cat, my own, so called, with deep affection, because he was almost red.

Mills's writing was charged—seared—by a keen awareness of human energy and disappointment, a passionate feeling for the human adventure, and a commitment to dignity. In many ways the style was the man. In a vigorous, instantly recognizable prose, he hammered home again and again the notion that people lived lives that were deeply shaped by social forces not of their own making, and that this irreducible fact had two consequences: it lent most human life a tragic aspect with a social root but created the potential—if only people saw a way forward—of improving life in a big way by concerted action.

In *The Sociological Imagination* and other works Mills insisted that a sociologist's proper subject was the intersection of biography and history. Mills invited, in other words, a personal approach to thought as well as a thoughtful approach to persons, so it was no fault of his that he came to be admired (and sometimes scorned) as a persona and not only a thinker, and that long after his death he still demands to be taken biographically as well as historically. In SDS we did not know Mills personally, for the most part, but (or therefore) a certain mystique flourished. It was said (accurately) that Mills was partial to motorcycles and that he lived in a house in the country that he had built himself. It was said (accurately) that he had been divorced more than once and (inaccurately) that he had been held back from a full professorship at Columbia because of his politics. If his personal life was unsettled, bohemian, and mainly *his own* in a manner equivalent to his intellectual journey and even his style, the fit seemed perfect.

Mills himself was not a man of political action apart from his writing, yet it was *as* a writer that he mattered, so his inclination to go it alone was far from a detriment. "I have been intellectually, politically, morally alone," he would write. "I have never known what others call 'fraternity' with any group, however small, neither academic nor political. With a few individuals, yes, I have known it, but with groups however small, no. . . . And the plain truth, so far as I know, is that I do not cry for it."[3] His own biography and history met in the distinctly American paradox first and most brilliantly personified by Ralph Waldo Emerson: the lone artisan who belongs by refusing to belong. "Intellectually and culturally I am as 'self-made' as it is possible to be," Mills wrote.[4] His "direction" was that "of the independent craftsman"—*craftsman* was one of his favorite words, borrowing, perhaps, from the "instinct of workmanship" derived from another great American frontiersman social scientist, Thorstein Veblen.[5]

Mills's forceful prose, his instinct for significant controversy, his Texas hell-for-leather aura, his reputation for intellectual fearlessness, and his passion for craftsmanship seemed all of a piece. A free intellectual tempted by action, he served as an engagé father or uncle figure, an outsider who counterposed himself not only to liberal academics who devoted themselves to explaining why radical change was either foreclosed or undesirable but also to the court intellectuals, the fawning men of power and quantification who clustered around the Kennedy administration and later helped anoint it Camelot. The Camelot insiders might speak of a New Frontier while living in glamour and reveling in power, while Mills, the loner, the antibureaucrat, was staking out a new frontier of his own.

II

Mills's output was huge in a short life, and here I can pick up only a few themes. He produced his strongest work in the fifties—*White Collar* (1951), *The Power Elite* (1956), *The Sociological Imagination* (1959)—banging up against political closure and cultural stupefaction. These books were, all in all, his major statements on what he liked to call "the big questions" about society, preceding the pamphlets, *The Causes of World War Three* (1958) and *Listen, Yankee: The Revolution in Cuba* (1960), along with an annotated collection, *The Marxists* (1962). (He also left a plethora of unfinished ambitious projects, some polemical, some deeply empirical.) A posthumous collection, *C. Wright Mills: Letters and Autobiographical Writings*, edited by Kathryn Mills with Pamela Mills, serves as a superb accompaniment to Mills's published books precisely because with him—as with Albert Camus, James Agee, and other exemplars of radical individualism—the personal and the political embraced each other so closely.

For all his debts to European social theory, one thing that stands out in the letters is Mills's raw Americanness. Growing up in Texas, schooled in Austin and Madison, living in Maryland and New York, Mills was full of frontier insouciance: "All this national boundary stuff is a kind of highway robbery, isn't it?"[6] "I am a Wobbly, personally, down deep and for good. . . . I take Wobbly to mean one thing: the opposite of bureaucrat."[7] In the midst of his activist pamphleteering, he still wrote: "I am a politician without a party"—or to put it another way, a party of one.[8] So it only reinforced Mills's reputation that he proved to be a martyr of a sort—not a casualty of jousts with political enemies but, in a certain sense, a casualty of his chosen way of life. This physically big, prepossessing, hard-driving man was more frail than he would want to let on or know. That he suffered a grave heart attack while feverishly preparing for his television debate on Latin American policy felt like a scene from *High Noon*, except that Gary Cooper is supposed to win the gunfight.

His prose was hard driving, the opposite of frail, and this was not incidental to his appeal. His writing was instantly recognizable, frequently emulated, and properly labeled muscular. It was frequently vivid and moving, often pointedly colloquial, though at times clumsy from an excess of deliberation (Mills worked hard for two decades to perfect his style). He was partial to collisions between nouns of action and nouns of failure—"showdown" and "thrust" versus "drift" and "default." He was partial to polemical categories like "crackpot realism" and "the military metaphysic." This style was, in the best sense of the word, masculine, though hardly macho—a macho writer would not be haunted by the prospect of mass violence or write that the "central goal of Western humanism [was] . . . the audacious control by reason of man's fate."9

Mills's willingness to go it alone ran deep. In a letter to the student newspaper at Texas A&M, written in his freshman year in the thick of the Great Depression, the nineteen-year-old Mills was asking: "Just who are the men with guts? They are the men . . . who have the imagination and the intelligence to formulate their own codes; the men who have the courage and the stamina to live their own lives in spite of social pressure and isolation."10 Rugged stuff, both democratic and noble, Whitmanian and Hemingwayesque, in a manner that has come to be mocked more than practiced or even read. A quarter of a century later the stance implied by the teenage Mills, which actually borrowed from the liberalism of John Stuart Mill, was called existentialism and, when transposed into a more urgent prose translated from the French, became the credo of teenage boys with the audacity to think they might change the world. Later this style was burlesqued as macho, brutal, distinctly (and pejoratively) "male." But the accusation of male exclusivity would miss something central to Mills's style, namely, the tenderness and longing that accompanied the urge to activity—qualities that carried a political hopefulness that was already unfashionable when Mills used it.11 To be precise, the spirit of these words was in the best sense adolescent.

I speak of adolescence here deliberately and without prejudice. The adult Mills himself commended the intensity and loyalty of adolescence: "I hope that I have not grown up. The whole notion of growing up is pernicious, and I am against it. To grow up means merely to lose the intellectual curiosity so many children and so few adults seem to have; to lose the strong attachments and rejections for other people so many adolescents and so few adults seem to have. . . . W. H. Auden recently put it very well: 'To grow up does not mean to outgrow either childhood or adolescence but to make use of them in an adult way.'"[12] Mills could never be dismissive about ideals or, in the dominant spirit of his time, consider idealism a psychiatric diagnosis. If he veered off toward the end of his life into black-and-white zones, sacrificing intellectual complexity for moralistic melodrama, he would probably have insisted that it was better to err in the direction of passionate intensity than gray judiciousness.

III

"I have never had occasion to take very seriously much of American sociology as such," Mills had the audacity to write in an application for a Guggenheim grant in 1944.[13] He told the foundation that he wrote for journals of opinion and "little magazines" because they took on the right topics "and even more because I wished to rid myself of a crippling academic prose and to develop an intelligible way of communicating modern social science to non-specialized publics." At twenty-eight the loner already wished to explain himself; the freelance politico wished to have on his side a reasoning public without letting it exact a suffocating conformity as the price of its support. Mills knew the difference between popularity, which he welcomed as a way to promote his ideas, and the desire to live a free life, which was irreducible, for (he wrote in a letter at forty) "way down deep and systematically I'm a goddamned anarchist."[14]

Not any old goddamned anarchist, however. Certainly not an intellectual slob. In his scholarly work he respected rigor, aspired to the high calling of craft, was usually unafraid of serious criticism and liked responding to it, liked the rough and tumble of straightforward dispute. Craft, not methodology—the distinction was crucial. Methodology was rigor mortis, dead rigor, rigor fossilized into esoterica of statistical practice that eclipsed the real stakes of research. Craft was work done with respect for materials, clarity about objectives, and a sense of the high drama and stakes of intellectual life. Craft partook of rigor, but rigor could not guarantee craft. A mastery of craft required not only technical knowledge and logic but a general curiosity, a Renaissance range of skills, a grasp of history and culture. It was the craft of sociological imagination, not a hyper-refinement of method made to appear scientific by declaring it "methodology," after all, that produced the other great sociological survival of the 1950s, *The Lonely Crowd*.

The Sociological Imagination (1959), Mills's most enduring book, ends with an appendix, "On Intellectual Craftsmanship," that in turn ends with these words (which, as it happens, I typed on an index card in college and posted next to my typewriter, hoping to live up to the spirit):

> Before you are through with any piece of work, no matter how indirectly on occasion, orient it to the central and continuing task of understanding the structure and the drift, the shaping and the meanings, of your own period, the terrible and magnificent world of human society in the second half of the twentieth century.[15]

Some mission for pale sociology!

Like *The Lonely Crowd,* Mills's major books were driven by large topics, not method or theory, yet they were also driven by a spirit of adventure. (He moved so far from the main line of sociology as to prefer the term *social studies* to *social sciences.*[16]) That a sociologist should work painstakingly, over the course of a career, to fill in a whole social picture should not seem as remarkable as it does today. In *The Sociological Imagination* Mills grandly excoriated the two dominant tendencies of mainstream sociology, the bloated puffery of Grand Theory and the microscopic marginality of Abstracted Empiricism, in terms that remain as important and vivid (and sometimes hilarious) today as they did more than forty years ago. All the more so, perhaps, because sociology has slipped still deeper into the troughs that Mills described. He would be amused at the way in which postmodernists, Marxists, and feminists have joined the former grandees of theory on their "useless heights,"[17] claiming high seriousness as well as usefulness for their pirouettes and performances, their monastic and masturbatory exercises, their populist cheerleading, political wishfulness, and self-importance. He would not have thought Theory a serious blow against irresponsible power. I think he would have recognized the pretensions of Theory as a class-bound ideology—that of a "new class," if you will—to be criticized just as he had exposed the supervisory ideology of the abstracted empiricists in their research teams, doing the intellectual busywork of corporate and government bureaucracies. I think he would also have recognized, in the grand intellectual claims and political bravado of Theory, a sort of Leninist assumption—a dangerous one—about the exalted mission of academics, as if, once they got their Theory straight, they would proclaim it to a waiting world and consider their work done.[18]

Of course, Mills had a high sense of mission himself—not only his own mission but that of intellectuals in general and social scientists in particular. He was committed to disciplined intellectual work guided by fidelity to what Max Weber (following the Lutheran spirit of faith) had called a "calling," a vocation in the original sense of being summoned by a voice. Not that Mills (who with Hans Gerth edited the first significant compilation of Weber's essays in English) agreed with Weber's conclusion that "science as a vocation" and "politics as a vocation," to name his two great essays on the subject, needed to be ruthlessly severed. Not at all. Mills thought the *questions* ought to come from values but the *answers* should not be rigged. A crucial difference. If the results of research made you grumpy, too bad. But he also thought that good social science became good politics when it moved into the open and generated public discussion. He came to this activist idea of intellectual life partly by temperament—he was not one to take matters lying down—but also by deduction and by elimination. For if intellectuals were not going to break the intellectual logjam, who would?

This was not, for Mills, a merely rhetorical question. It was a question that, in the Deweyan pragmatic spirit that had been the subject of his doctoral dissertation, required an experimental answer, an answer that would unfold in real life through reflection upon experience. For his conclusion after a decade of work was that if one were looking for a fusion of reason and power—at least potential power—there was nowhere else to look but to intellectuals. Mills had sorted through the available history makers in his books of the late 1940s and 1950s—labor in *The New Men of Power,* the middle classes in *White Collar,* and the chiefs of top institutions themselves in *The Power Elite.* Labor was not up to the challenge of structural reform, white-collar employees were confused and rearguard, and the power elite was irresponsible. Mills concluded that intellectuals and only intellectuals had a fighting chance to deploy reason. Because they could embody reason in addressing social problems when no one else could do so, it was incumbent upon them to try, in addressing a problem, to have "a view of the strategic points of intervention—of the 'levers' by which the structure may be maintained or changed; and an assessment of those who are in a position to intervene but are not doing so."[19]

As he would write in *The Marxists,* a political philosophy had to encompass not only an analysis of society and a set of theories of how it works but "an ethic, an articulation of *ideals.*"[20] It followed that intellectuals should be explicit about their values and rigorous in considering contrary positions. It also followed that research work should be supplemented by blunt writing that was meant to inform and mobilize what he called, following John Dewey, "publics." In Mills's words, "The educational and the political role of social science in a democracy is to help cultivate and sustain publics and individuals that are able to develop, to live with, and to act upon adequate definitions of personal and social realities."[21]

To a degree that only later came to seem controversial, Mills credited reason—and its attainability, even as a glimmering goal that could never be reached but could be approximated ever more closely, asymptotically. He wrote about the Enlightenment without a sneer.[22] He thought the problem with the condition of the Enlightenment at midcentury was not that we had too much Enlightenment but that we had too little, and the tragedy was that the universal genuflection to technical rationality—in the form of scientific research, business calculation, and state planning—

was the perfect disguise for this great default. The democratic self-governance of rational men and women was damaged partly by the bureaucratization of the economy and the state. (This was a restatement of Weber's great discovery: that increased rationality *of institutions* made for less freedom, or least no more freedom, *of individuals*.) And democratic prospects were damaged, too—in ways that Mills was trying to work out when he died—because the West was coping poorly with the entry of the "underdeveloped" countries onto the world stage, and because neither liberalism (which had, in the main, degenerated into techniques of "liberal practicality") nor Marxism (which had, in the main, degenerated into a blind doctrine that rationalized tyranny) could address their urgent needs. "Our major orientations—liberalism and socialism—have virtually collapsed as adequate explanations of the world and of ourselves," he wrote.[23] This was dead on.

IV

Forty-five years is a long time in the social sciences (or, better, social studies). Not only does society change but so do scholarly procedures. The cycle of generations alone would guarantee some disciplinary change, for each generation of young scholars must carve out new niches in order to distinguish itself from its predecessor, and the material from which young scholars must carve is the old discipline itself. So do styles and vocabulary transmute, so do the governing paradigms turn over. In the 1940s and 1950s, when Mills wrote, and through the 1960s, administrative research was a growth industry; Mills accordingly singled it out for attention—and scorn—in *The Sociological Imagination*. In the thick of the Cold War, Abstracted Empiricism was useful not only to corporations but to government agencies. But the money ran out, as did the confidence in government-sponsored planning and what Mills called "liberal practicality." Accordingly, today's Abstracted Empiricism is not as prestigious as in Mills's days. Likewise, the Grand Theory that would make him chortle today would less likely be Talcott Parsons's than Michel Foucault's, in which power, having been virtually nothing in the structural-functionalism of the 1950s, turns out to be everything.

This makes it all the more remarkable that most of *The Sociological Imagination* remains as valid, and necessary, as ever. In 1959 Mills identified the main directions of sociology in terms largely valid today: "a set of bureaucratic techniques which inhibit social inquiry by methodological pretensions, which congest such work by obscurantist conceptions, or which trivialize it by concern with minor problems unconnected with publicly relevant issues."[24] It remains true, as he noted in defending the high purpose of sociology, that literature, art, and criticism largely fail to bring intellectual clarity to social life.[25] The sense of political limbo is once again palpable. In the West, as Mills wrote, "the frequent absence of engaging legitimation and the prevalence of mass apathy are surely two of the central political facts."[26] "Prosperity," however unequally distributed (and it is far more unequal today than in 1959), once again presents itself as the all-purpose solution to all social questions. Unfortunately, these declarations of Mills's have proved largely prophetic.

Still, four and a half decades are four and a half decades—the length of Mills's life—and, not surprisingly, tangible social changes require that his outlook be updated. First, Mills was concerned about hidden authority, tacit, veiled, and therefore not controversial in public life. In the muddle of Eisenhower's America the clustering of powerful corporations did not meet with much cogent criticism. (Recall that *The Sociological Imagination* was published more than a year before Eisenhower warned against the "military-industrial complex.") The left was defunct, the right more preoccupied with the dangers of communism than the usurpation of power by centralized institutions. Moreover, the population was largely content with the reigning combination of affluence and Cold War. When government power intervened to build interstate highways, finance suburbs, or subsidize research universities, few objected.

Today, authorities of all sorts are more likely to be suspected, mocked, and scorned than invisible. The Cold War is no longer available as a rationale for government power, though the war on terrorism has emerged as a surrogate framework. As a result of the cultural upheavals of the 1960s and the uninterrupted fascination with personal liberation through commodities, what has become normal is disrespect for almost all institutions and traditions—the branches of government, business, labor, the media, the professions. Such political faith as there is honors the mythology of the market, an institution that is more a mystique than a firm structure, since it represents the coexistence of many partial institutions—including government preferences and subsidies. The ideological wars pit fundamentalist reverence against the anti-institutional liberalism that Robert Bellah and his colleagues have called "expressive individualism."[27] Since the Vietnam War, Watergate, and the elections of Ronald Reagan and George W. Bush, the faith in liberal practicality that Mills sought to overcome has been considerably tarnished, since government action has been largely delegitimized except when police and incarceration are at issue or local pork barrels remain to be disgorged.

Today, too, it cannot be said—in the words of *The Sociological Imagination*—that "much private uneasiness goes unformulated."[28] To the contrary. In the United States complacency about most social arrangements curiously coexists with widespread anxiety about them—or rather, anxieties in the plural, since the varieties of dissatisfaction and estrangement do not coalesce around a single axis of conflict. To the extent that "malaise and indifference . . . form the social and personal climate of contemporary American society," they coexist with many dispersed antagonisms, a vast proliferation of interest groups and labels with which Americans believe they can name those responsible for their troubles.[29] For conservatives it is the liberal media, or secular humanism, or moral relativism, or a breakdown of patriotism, or uppity minorities. For liberals it is the conservative media, or resurgent capital, or racism, or market ideology paid for by right-wing foundations. For feminists it is patriarchy; for patriarchs, feminism. When *The Sociological Imagination* was published, public demonstrations were jarringly uncommon; today, they are everyday. Expressions of political sentiment have been professionalized, organized through the technologies of opinion mobilization. The insurgencies of the 1960s, having succeeded in taking up Mills's call to convert private troubles to public issues, have often been plasticized into "Astroturf" and "grass-tops" pseudo-movements.

Hopeful about a revival of democratic engagement, Mills did not fully appreciate just how much enthusiasm Americans could bring to acquiring and using consumer goods. He underestimated the degree to which, starting in the late 1960s, majorities in a democratic society would find satisfactions, even provisional identities or clusters of identities, in the proliferation of commodities produced for the market. His America was still sheltered from hedonism by the Puritan overhang of the work ethic. Still, he did prefigure one of the striking ideas of perhaps his most formidable antagonist, Daniel Bell—namely, the centrality, in corporate capitalism, of the tension between getting (via the Protestant ethic) and spending (via the hedonistic ethic).[30] Mills would have been struck by the fact that most Americans not only have money to spend, or are willing to borrow it, but that they have channeled the spirit of fun and leisure into technological wizardry. Still, he did pioneering work on the institutionalization of popular culture. The chapter on celebrities in *The Power Elite* is one of the first major approaches in the history of sociology to their ascendancy.

Which brings me to another transformation postdating 1959, namely, the growing presence of the media—not only what used to be called the mass media, with single corporate senders beaming their signals to tens of millions of receivers, but the whole dynamic, synergistic welter of television, radio, magazines, toys, the Internet, the Walkman, linking up multinational conglomerates with demographic niches, saturating daily experience in manifold ways, and, in sum, taking up a vast portion of public attention. This transformation, still under way, requires a new application of the sociological imagination, as Mills well knew. (His projected volume on "the cultural apparatus" was a casualty of his untimely death.) Amid the enormity of popular culture he would have been aghast, but not surprised, to see how the language of private life has penetrated into conflicts of public value. It remains true, in Mills's words, that "many great public issues as well as many private troubles are described in terms of 'the psychiatric.'"[31] If today "the psychiatric" is less likely to be discussed in psychoanalytic terms and more likely in the language of self-help, twelve-step programs, confessions, and the like—as on television talk shows—this is nonetheless not what Mills meant by the conversion of private troubles to public issues; it is more the other way round.

Mills also did not sufficiently apply himself to the vexing central problem of race. He hated racism, but though he lived through the early years of the civil rights movement, he wrote surprisingly little about the dynamics of race in U.S. life. The students of the civil rights movement interested him as one of many groupings of young intellectuals rising into history around the globe, but the way in which racial identification shaped and distorted people's life chances did not loom large for him. Today, race has become so salient in U.S. social structure and discourse as, at times, to drown out other contending forces. Since Mills's death other dimensions of identity have also reared up in importance—as scales sorting out privileges and opportunities, and as prisms refracting reality, bending the rays of light that Americans (and others) use to see the world. Sex and sexuality, religion, and region, in addition to class, are other factors that the sociological imagination today must reckon with, and centrally. Such advances as sociology has made since the 1950s, in fact, emerge precisely here: in analyses of the dynamics of sex and gender, of race and ethnicity, some of them inspired by Mills's own call to understand private troubles as public issues.

A curious fact about contemporary culture is that sociological language has, in many ways, become a normal element in commonplace talk as well as political speech, though often in a degraded form. By a dreary irony of a spongy culture, the sociological gloss on ephemeral events is, by now, a routine component of popular journalism. This is, in part, a tribute to the success of sociology in entering the academic curriculum. Journalists and editors have taken the courses and learned to talk the talk; they are no longer confident that, without expertise, they can follow the main contours of social change.[32] But the result is that, in popular conversation and in the media, as in the academy and the behind-the-scenes work of advertising agencies and political consultants, the sociological imagination has been trivialized by success. Not a commercial movie or toy or television series succeeds today without commentary springing up to "explain" its success with references to the "strains" and "insecurities" of the contemporary era. Corporations hire consultants to anticipate, or shape, demand with the benefit of a once-over-lightly reading of social trends. I am frequently called upon to make such divinations in sociological lingo, and I have watched the media appetite for plausible-sounding, expert-delivered tidbits stretch since the 1980s to become a staple of conventional entertainment coverage. What does it mean that two movies of type X are suddenly hits or that a new toy or fashion or term or candidate is hot? In the media a pass at sociological understanding became an acceptable—eventually, almost obligatory—element in the trend story, certifying the reportage (however unwarrantedly) as something more serious than fan gossip. The same happened in the field of cultural studies, where popular ephemera were elevated to objects worthy of the most ponderous scrutiny.[33] Pop sociology is sociological imagination lite, a fast-food version of nutriment, a sprinkling of holy water on the commercial trend of the moment, and a trivialization of insight.

V

It goes without saying that Mills felt urgently about the state of the world—a sentiment that needed no excuse during the Cold War, though one needs reminders today of just how realistic and uncrackpot it was to sound the alarm about the sheer world-incinerating power that had been gathered into the hands of Washington's national security establishment and its Soviet counterpart. It cannot be overemphasized that much of Mills's work on power was specific to a historical situation that can be described succinctly: the existence of national strategies for nuclear war. Mills declared intermittently in *The Power Elite*, and more bluntly in *The Causes of World War Three*, that the major reason that America's most powerful should be considered dangerous was that they controlled weapons of mass destruction and were in a position not only to contemplate their use but to launch them. Mills's judgment on this score was as acute as it was simple: "Ours is not so much a time of big decisions as a time for big decisions that are not being made. A lot of bad little decisions are crippling the chances for the appropriate big ones."[34] Most demurrers missed this essential point.[35] To head off pluralist critics Mills acknowledged that there were policy clashes of local and sectoral groups, medium-size business, labor, professions, and others, producing "a semiorganized stalemate," but he thought the noisy visible conflicts took place mainly at "the middle level of power."[36] As for domestic questions, Mills exaggerated the unanimity of powerful groupings. He was extrapolating from the prosperous, post–New Deal, liberal-statist consensus that united Truman, Eisenhower, and Kennedy more than it divided them. Like most observers of the fifties, Mills underestimated the potential for a conservative movement.[37] But about the centralization of power where it counted most, he was far more right than wrong.

One has to recall the setting. Mills died a mere seven months before the Cuban Missile Crisis came within a hair's breadth of triggering a nuclear war. Khrushchev's reckless shipment of missiles to Cuba triggered the momentous White House decisions of October 1962. Enough time has passed since then without thermonuclear war that an elementary point has to be underscored: the decision of Kennedy's inner circle to back down from the brink of war was not inevitable. It was, shall we say, contingent rather than structural. A handful of men—they *were* men—had full opportunity to make the wrong decision and incinerate millions. They made the right decision, as did Khrushchev, in the end, and the superpowers clambered back from the precipice. At that world-shattering moment when eyeballs faced eyeballs, the men in charge had the wisdom not to blow their eyeballs and millions of other people's away. *They had the opportunity and the means to make other decisions. They were hair-raisingly close.* That they did not make the wrong decisions does not detract from Mills's good judgment in taking seriously this huge fact about the U.S. elite: they were heading toward a crossroads where they might well have made a momentous, irreversible wrong turn. Who these men were, how they got to their commanding positions, how there had turned out to be so much at stake in their choices—there could be no more important subject for social science. Whatever the failings of Mills's arguments in *The Power Elite,* his central point obtained: the power to launch a vastly murderous war existed, in concentrated form. This immense fact no paeans to pluralism could dilute.

Mills not only invoked the sociological imagination, he practiced it brilliantly if partially. Careful critics like David Riesman, who thought Mills's picture of white-collar workers too monolithically gloomy, still acknowledged the insight of his portraits and the soundness of his research.[38] Even the polemical voice of a Cuban revolutionary that Mills adopted in *Listen, Yankee*—a voice he thought that Americans, "shot through with hysteria," were crazy to ignore—was quietly shaped by Mills's ability to grasp where, from what milieu, such a revolutionary was coming from.[39] In a sense, Mills's stirring invocation to student movements at the turn of the sixties stemmed from this affirming side of his sociological imagination, too. He was deeply attuned to the growth of higher education and the growing importance of science in the military-corporate world. More than any other sociologist of the time, Mills anticipated the ways in which conventional careers and narrow life plans within and alongside the military-industrial complex would fail to satisfy a growing proto-elite of students trained to take their places in an establishment unworthy of their moral vision. If he exaggerated the significance—or goodness—of intellectuals as a social force, and underestimated the force of a conservative recoil that had barely begun to show itself at the time of his death, this was also a by-product of his faith in the powers of reason. Believing that human beings learn as they live, he was on the side of improvement through reflection. Thus he thought that Castro's tyranny, and other harsh features of the Cuban revolution, were "part of a phase, and that I and other North Americans should help the Cubans pass *through* it."[40] In his last months he was increasingly disturbed about Fidel Castro's trajectory toward Soviet-style "socialism" and restive in the vanishing middle ground. Two fates afflicted free-minded radicals in the twentieth century: to be universally contrarian and end up on the sidelines or to hope against hope that the next revolution would invent a new wheel. On the strength of Mills's letters, my guess is that he would have passed through the second fate to the first yet without reconciling himself to the sidelines.

Of course, no one can know where Mills might have gone as the student movement radicalized, grew more militant, more culturally estranged, reckless, and self-destructive, partly from desperation, partly from arrogant self-inflation. Of the generation of intellectuals who thrived in the fifties, Mills more than any other was in a position to grasp not only the strength of what was happening among students, blacks, and women but also the wrong-headedness and tragedy; he might have spoken of it, argued for the best and against the worst, in a voice that would have been hard to ignore—though it would probably have been ignored anyway. I think it likely that, had he lived, he would have said about the New Left what he wrote in 1960 about the Cuban Revolution: *"I do not worry about it, I worry for it and with it."* [41]

For all that his life was cut short, more of Mills's work endures than that of any other critic of his time. His was an indispensable brilliant voice in sociology and social criticism—and in the difficult, necessary effort to link the two. He was a restless, engaged, engaging moralist, asking the big questions, keeping open the sense of what an intellectual's life might be. His work is bracing, often thrilling, even when one disagrees. One reads and rereads with a feeling of being challenged beyond one's received wisdom, called to one's best thinking, one's highest order of judgment. For an intellectual of our time, no higher praise is possible.

Notes

1. In referring to "exhausted ideologies," I am deliberately using a word from the little-noted subtitle of Daniel Bell's *The End of Ideology: On the Exhaustion of Political Ideas in the Fifties* (Glencoe, Ill.: Free Press, 1960).

2. His debate opponent was to have been A. A. Berle Jr., who was not only a top adviser on Latin America to President Kennedy but also a major exponent of the view that management in the modern corporation had taken control from stock owners. Mills had criticized Berle, the influential coauthor of *The Modern Cor-*

poration and *Private Property* (New York: Macmillan, 1933), for his views of corporate conscience (Mills, *The Power Elite* [New York: Oxford University Press, 1956], pp. 125n, 126n). For those who knew this history, the forthcoming debate looked even more like a showdown.

3. From an essay in the form of a letter written in the fall of 1957 and addressed to "Tovarich," whom Mills imagined as a symbolic Russian opposite number. *C. Wright Mills: Letters and Autobiographical Writings*, edited by Kathryn Mills with Pamela Mills (Berkeley: University of California Press, 2000), p. 250.

4. Mills, "To Tovarich," fall 1957, p. 29.

5. Ibid., p. 252.

6. Ibid., p. 26.

7. Ibid., p. 252.

8. Mills note in a notebook intended for "Tovarich," June 1960, p. 303.

9. Mills, *The Causes of World War Three* (New York: Ballantine, 1958), pp. 185–86.

10. Letter to editor, *Battalion*, April 3, 1935, in *C. Wright Mills*, p. 34.

11. Paul Goodman, another exemplary public intellectual who inspired the New Left, later wrote a piece for the *New York Review of Books* (December 30, 1971) on what he called "the sweet style of Ernest Hemingway," just as the strong silent style was about to pass into the netherworld, thanks to Kate Millett and other feminists. Goodman, even more than Mills, practiced an instantly recognizable prose style that found grace in lumbering.

12. Mills, "To Tovarich," fall 1957, p. 248.

13. Mills to John Simon Guggenheim Memorial Foundation, November 7, 1944, *C. Wright Mills*, pp. 83–84. To the credit of the foundation, he got the grant. This would make for an interesting subject: the way in which, while sociology was hardening into the molds Mills righteously scorned, it had not altogether hardened—which permitted the leaders of the field to honor Mills and take him seriously, at least in his early work, while recoiling from his later.

14. Mills to Harvey and Bette Swados, November 3, 1956, in *C. Wright Mills*, p. 217–18.

15. Mills, *The Sociological Imagination* (New York: Oxford University Press, 1959), p. 225.

16. Ibid., p. 18n.

17. Ibid., p. 33.

18. I have elaborated on the implied politics of the Theory Class in "Sociology for Whom? Criticism for Whom?" in Herbert J. Gans, ed., *Sociology in America* (Newbury Park, Calif.: Sage, 1990), pp. 214–26.

19. Mills, *The Sociological Imagination*, p. 131.

20. Mills, *The Marxists* (New York: Dell, 1962), p. 12, emphasis in original.

21. Mills, *The Sociological Imagination*, p. 192.

22. See the great chapter "On Reason and Freedom," in Mills, *The Sociological Imagination*, pp. 165–76.

23. Mills, *The Sociological Imagination*, p. 166.

24. Ibid., p. 20.

25. Ibid., p. 18.

26. Ibid., p. 41.

27. Robert N. Bellah et al., *Habits of the Heart: Individualism and Commitment in American Life* (New York: Harper and Row, 1985).

28. Mills, *The Sociological Imagination*, p. 12.

29. Ibid., pp. 12–13.

30. Bell, *The Cultural Contradictions of Capitalism* (New York: Basic Books, 1976). For one of many examples of Mills's anticipating this important argument, see *The Power Elite* (1956; reprint, New York: Oxford University Press, 2000), p. 384. Bell wrote a scathing critique of *The Power Elite* (the review is reprinted as "Is There a Ruling Class in America? The Power Elite Reconsidered," chap. 3 in *The End of Ideology*), properly chastising Mills for scanting the differences between New Deal and Republican administrations but also charging him—in the middle of the twentieth century!—with an overemphasis on power as violence. Mills dismissed "Mr. Bell's debater's points" in a letter to Hans Gerth of December 2, 1958, writing that he would not deign to respond publicly (*C. Wright Mills*, p. 268). This is too bad, because Mills could have straightforwardly and convincingly rebutted most of Bell's points.

31. Mills, *The Sociological Imagination*, p. 12.

32. On the popularization of sociological terms, see Dennis H. Wrong, "The Influence of Sociological Ideas on American Culture," in Gans, *Sociology in America*, pp. 19–30.

33. See chapter 5, "The Antipolitical Populism of Cultural Studies."

34. Mills, *The Causes of World War Three*, p. 21.

35. Irving Howe's harsh critique of *The Causes of World War Three* (*Dissent*, spring 1959, pp. 191–96) berated Mills for claiming that the United States and Soviet Union were converging into a "fearful symmetry" (*Causes*, p. 9). Howe charged Mills with coming "un-

comfortably close" to defending "a kind of 'moral coexistence'" (pp. 195–96), and the two men broke off their relations after the review appeared. In fury at the complacency of U.S. leadership, Mills did at times veer toward the cavalier. Despite his sympathy for East European dissidents, Mills could indeed be, as Howe charged, slapdash about Soviet imperialism in the satellite countries. But subsequent scholarship makes plain just how great was the U.S. lead over the Soviet nuclear establishment in the late 1950s, when Mills was writing, how fraudulent was Kennedy's claim of a "missile gap," and therefore how much greater was the U.S. responsibility to back down from nuclear strategies that could easily have eventuated in an exterminating war.

36. Mills, *The Causes of World War Three*, p. 39.

37. In the chapter called "The Conservative Mood" in *The Power Elite*, Mills did write that "the conservative mood is strong, almost as strong as the pervasive liberal rhetoric" (p. 331), but he did not anticipate that opposition to civil rights and general antistatism might fuse into popular movements that would eventually take over the Republican Party.

38. Riesman, review of *White Collar*, *American Journal of Sociology* 16 (1951): 513–15. Mills's "middle levels of power" was a concept aimed directly at Riesman's "veto groups" in *The Lonely Crowd*. Despite their analytical differences, however, Riesman was devoutly antinationalist, and his active commitment to the peace movement of the early 1960s converged at many points with Mills's suspicion of the power elite.

39. Mills, *Listen, Yankee* (New York: Ballantine, 1960), p. 179.

40. Ibid., p. 183, emphasis in original. It should be remembered that his misjudgments came early in the revolution. He wrote, for example: "The Cuban revolution, unlike the Russian, has, in my judgment, solved the major problems of agricultural production by its agrarian reform" (*Listen, Yankee*, p. 185). Such are the perils of pamphleteering.

41. Ibid., p. 179, emphasis in original.

3

Irving Howe's Partition

I

Irving Howe edited the left-wing quarterly *Dissent* for more than thirty-eight years. He had coeditors, but *Dissent* was *his* magazine: he was its public face and it was his primary outlet. He was, at the same time, probably the most prolific literary critic of his generation, the one most attuned to political surroundings, to the burdens that they placed on writers, and to the possibilities that they opened up. Yet his criticism hardly ever appeared in his own magazine. It was as if he had two sets of relatives, loved them both, but knew better than to seat them at the same dinner table.

Around 1990, not long after I joined the editorial board of *Dissent,* I told him that I thought the journal should publish literary criticism, cultural commentary, even a poem or short story now and then. He grimaced. "No, once we start publishing poems, the mailbox will never be empty. We'll get hundreds, none of them good, and we'll still have to read them. I don't want to have to write to a shop steward in Detroit explaining why we don't want to publish his bad poem." Once he had published a bad poem by a political hero (I forget who) simply to honor the author. The circumstance was special, but he still felt some embarrassment at having made any exceptions. I respected his arguments but pressed the case a bit further. If the left was going to be not just a place for confirmed politicos but a sort of ideological home, I argued, the journal had to be a place that felt more encompass-ing—"a world more attractive," in the title of one of his essay collections. No, no, Irving said, there were other places for that. *Dissent* needed to focus on what it did best, what it was indis-pensable for. The literature and criticism that the journal could attract would not be the best. Perhaps he knew that his own rare exceptions published in *Dissent* were not his strongest work. He sounded as if he had made this case before. (In fact he had done so, to the young editor Brian Morton, among others.[1]) Each rep-etition only hardened Irving's rejection of sentimentalism. So we left the matter.

It was striking: America's best-known left-wing critic, one of its most celebrated critics of any persuasion, explaining why the literature he loved with a fierce burning love, and the criticism he practiced as his profession—his calling, actually—should be kept out of his own magazine.

As much as he was committed to analytical intelligence, Irving was equally committed to good writing. He worked hard to get sentences right. His own work he edited unprotectively, and when he gathered his articles into book form, he was still fiddling with individual words. He was a gifted polemicist even in a generation of gifted polemicists (early Trotskyism did not hurt) who strained hard to purify his style, strip it of ornament, even of the brilliance that he identified, with decided ambivalence, as the characteris-tic manner of the New York intellectuals. (This style, which for a while qualified as a cult, was "highly self-conscious . . . with an unashamed vibration of bravura and display, . . . nervous, strewn with knotty or flashy phrases, impatient with transitions and oth-er concessions to dullness, willfully calling attention to itself . . . fond of rapid twists, taking pleasure in dispute, dialectic, dazzle," conveying, at its best, a view of the intellectual life as "free-lance dash, peacock strut, daring hypothesis, knockabout synthesis" but at bottom "a sign that writers were offering not their work or ideas but their persona as content."[2]) In his thirties he was already be-ginning to aspire to the plain style commended by his beloved George Orwell. On me and other younger writers, he urged direct-ness: trim those adjectives! (For a while I had a penchant for three in a row. He knocked them back to two. He was right.)

Accessibility was a democratic responsibility, so plainness was a political act. But literature had a different obligation: to excavate beneath the level of consciousness. Literature might well sabotage the author's intentions. So the literary act subverted reason. It was always, irreducibly, dangerous—an interference with the strategic hope and rational prayer of political advocacy. As Brian Morton has put it, "Irving saw politics as the realm of responsibility, literature as a realm where eruptions from the unconscious were not only permissible but necessary."[3] What needed saying was at odds with what was good to say. Imagination, he wrote, is "implicit in the literary act." "The novelist's risk" was "that the imagination will bring to awareness more than he means it to."[4] This is not a new thought. But it has a special poignancy in the work of a man who was equally committed to the socialist's reason and the novelist's risk.

Moreover, the literary appraisal might work against one's fealty to truth or justice. Up through his last essays, he repeatedly wrestled with the problem of the tension between literary achievement and the novelist's political values. Again and again he acknowledged facing what he called "a severe problem, some would say confusion: How can you say that *The Possessed* is both a great work of literature and also a work that offers a distorted, even malicious treatment of its subject?" In his late manner of facing difficulties bluntly, he went on: "How to answer this question I am not at all sure: perhaps by recognizing that the imperatives of literature and history are at deep variance."[5]

Deep conflicts of value are not rare. An industrial polluter amasses a great art collection. A war criminal is charming. To acknowledge such "deep variances" is to reconcile oneself to the multiplicity and incommensurability of human realms. There are no straight lines in human affairs, no formulas for making the crooked straight. It is a mark of literary sensibility, perhaps, to abide these conflicts, even to relish them, rather than seeking to overcome, let alone dissolve, them. A novelist is not in the business of cutting Gordian knots but lovingly traces the string in its twists and turns. What's tracery for the novelist is also tracery for the critic. Howe concluded this discussion: "In any case, I am entangled in this difficulty, and the tangle is exactly where I want to remain, since I believe it is faithful to the actual experience of reading such novels."[6] Writing in his critical persona, he defended his view not morally or politically but on the ground of literary experience. Literary power trumped historical infidelity as it might just as easily eclipse a character's (or the novelist's) moral iniquity. You could not maximize all values at one time and place, and you should not try. Yet again the place to honor such conflicts was in your critical writing, not in your political magazine.

If anything, criticism pursues higher values than politics does. Criticism cherishes an aesthetic in which the crooked cannot be made straight. The overriding principle is fidelity to contradiction. This may well require not only unearthing an irreducible conflict but deepening it. What it assuredly does not require is resolving the conflict. Here, too, criticism is like literature. The epigraph to *Politics and the Novel* comes from Max Scheler: true tragedy arises "when the idea of 'justice' appears to be leading to the destruction of higher values."[7] Such tragedy is sublime—obviously, a literary judgment, not a practical commendation. Tragedy can hardly be the objective of politics (though it may well be the result).

Howe, in other words, honored two gods by separating them. Like any sensible child of two incompatible, envious, and demanding parents, he made his peace by rendering to each what each was due, cautioning against judging "one area of experience in terms of another, which is almost always a dangerous kind of judgment to make."[8]

So to segregate literary-critical from political work helped Howe to order his life. In his own books he could mix his realms, while *Dissent* would keep his politics fenced off. But I discern another reason, deeper, more personal, why he partitioned his commitments. It can be found in some of his critical observations themselves. In literature he disapproved of excessive control. He liked the friction of the unexpected against the system. He had kind words for great writers—Dostoyevsky and Hardy, particularly—who are partial to astounding coincidences, coincidences that decisively jolt their plots, as long as such moments feel like eruptions in the grain of everyday life rather than products of the author's ideological scheme. Once when I praised Cynthia

Ozick's *The Messiah of Stockholm,* he deplored the puppeteer that he saw managing her plot. In an essay on Flannery O'Connor he writes approvingly of—indeed he "find[s] himself moved by"— moments in fiction when the "unexpected happens, a perception, an insight, a confrontation which may not be in accord with the writer's original intention and may not be strictly required by the logic of the action, but which nevertheless caps the entire story. This moment of revelation gains part of its power from a sharp and sudden brush against the writer's evident plan of meaning—it calls into question all 'structural analysis'; the writer seems to be shaken by the demands of his own imagination, so that the material of the story 'acts back' upon him."9 In some of O'Connor's work he spots an ideological (in her case, Catholic) mechanism at work, but in a lesser-known story, "Revelation," he approves of her "vision of irremediable disorder." Here she does not duck the irrational depths with "the kind of last-minute acquisition of understanding with which literature has so often tried to get around life."10 Here she has the courage of the holes or antinomies in her convictions.

But these are moments he wants *in books.* He does not want them in the flesh and he does not want them in politics. There, they unnerve him.

II

Howe wrote voluminously on the politics of literature, most systematically in his 1957 book *Politics and the Novel,* where he succeeded best in letting his passions rub up against each other. But almost without exception—a note on Silone here, a tribute to East European dissident writers there—he kept *Dissent* clear. On the rare occasion when Howe mixed realms and imported his literary criticism into his political magazine, the result was not happy. Politics trumped literature.

"Black Boys and Native Sons," published in *Dissent* in the fall of 1963, displayed the critic as border guard, issuing visas for literature. Irving's chief culprit was James Baldwin, who had sought, in an essay called "Everybody's Protest Novel," to disburden himself of the assumption that an African American writer must serve as a political—indeed, racial—ambassador. The world, the young Baldwin wrote (he was twenty-five when he first published in a 1949 issue of *Partisan Review*), "tends to trap and immobilize you in the role you play"; he hoped "to prevent myself from becoming merely a Negro; or even, merely a Negro writer." What Baldwin conceived as refuge, Howe conceived as delusion. As we shall see in a moment, he campaigned persistently—obsessively—against the presumptions of the self-made man of action. He scorned the romance of self-creation as defended by Baldwin and embodied by Ralph Ellison in *Invisible Man*, a novel that Howe had considered "brilliant though flawed" in a largely favorable review published in *The Nation* in 1952. The novel's chief flaw, he wrote then, was

> the hero's discovery [toward the end of the book] that "my world has become one of infinite possibilities," his refusal to be the "invisible man" whose body is manipulated by various social groups. Though the unqualified assertion of self-liberation was a favorite strategy among American literary people in the fifties, it is also vapid and insubstantial. It violates the reality of social life, the interplay between external conditions and personal will, quite as much as the determinism of the thirties. The unfortunate fact remains that to define one's individuality is to stumble upon social barriers which stand in the way, all too much in the way, of "infinite possibilities." Freedom can be fought for, but it cannot always be willed or asserted into existence. And it seems hardly an accident that even as Ellison's hero asserts the "infinite possibilities," he makes no attempt to specify them.[11]

Against such willed and fanciful declarations of freedom, Howe sided with the Richard Wright of *Native Son*, whose naturalism, however limited as a literary form, at least refrained from false promises. Wright, Howe maintained, was admirable because he told the necessary truth about black experience and the costs of racism. "What, then, was the experience of a man with a black skin, what could it be in this country?" Howe asked. "How could a Negro put pen to paper, how could he so much as think or breathe, without some impulsion to protest, be it harsh or mild, political or private, released or buried?"

To the contrary, he wrote, Baldwin "evades, through rhetorical sweep, the genuinely difficult issue of the relationship between social experience and literature."[12] Curiously, Howe here violated his own literary standards. If this issue was "genuinely difficult," it was also too difficult to be solved by the literary formula: add protest to realism. Under ordinary circumstances this formula defeats literature. It is literature's bear trap. Indeed, in other settings Howe vividly dismissed programmatic writing. In his book on Thomas Hardy, Howe referred to "literary tact" as the solution to "the most difficult and elusive problem faced by a writer: to what extent should he yield himself to his unavoidable urge for shaping his work in accordance with his beliefs, and to what extent should he resist that urge in favor of the autonomy of the world, the *difference* of everything beyond his self?"[13] His admiration for Hardy's equipoise was boundless. Why couldn't Howe muster such admiration for Baldwin's prose at its most delicate?

Partly, he tells us, because he suspected its "brilliance of gesture"[14]—as we have seen, a glitter that Howe suspected was really a proof of intellectual fool's gold. But this cannot be the whole story, cannot account for the odd fact that he was violating his own strictures and publishing this essay in *Dissent* in the first place. Why did he break his own rule? And why at this juncture (when Baldwin's essays dated from more than a decade before, and *Invisible Man* from 1952, and Howe's own writings about both, recycled verbatim in the *Dissent* of 1963, from 1952 and 1962, respectively)? There is a mystery.

But note the historical moment. It was 1963: the civil rights movement was surging. Howe's essay appeared just after the momentous March on Washington for Jobs and Freedom. In the Negro—soon to be black—revolt James Baldwin was not only an important writer, he was the single most visible black intellectual. No longer published in little magazines like *Partisan Review,* he now heralded, from the unexpected pulpit of the *New Yorker,* "the fire next time"—the name of one of those essays where Baldwin, Howe wrote, reached "heights of passionate exhortation unmatched in modern American writing," with "a grave and sustained eloquence."[15] Baldwin had heard the call of the moment and graduated from the baroque and "somewhat lacquered" intricacy of the young essayist to the declamatory mode of the public spokesman, making him "one of the two or three greatest essayists this country has ever produced."[16]

In the process, however, Baldwin now fell into Richard Wright's dilemma. "One generation passes its dilemmas to the next." It would no longer do for Baldwin to dismiss the strenuous, militant spokesman role cavalierly. He must "struggle with militancy"[17]—an odd infelicity, or perhaps an unintentional indication that Howe didn't know whether he wanted to call Baldwin a militant or to declare that militancy poses problems with which a writer must struggle. In any case Baldwin now ran the risk of collapsing into politics with an unwarranted coarsening certitude. To run that risk was, to use the title of a later Baldwin book, "the price of the ticket" whenever a writer took to the soapbox. Astutely, Howe noted that "Baldwin's most recent essays are shot through with intellectual confusion, torn by the conflict between his assumption that the Negro must find an honorable place in the life of American society and his apocalyptic sense, mostly fear but just a little hope, that this society is beyond salvation, doomed with the sickness of the West."[18]

Historical moments do not stand up on their hind legs and announce themselves in their own voices. They require interpreters—indeed, we recognize (or misrecognize) their sound and shape only because interpreters name them (and quarrel about the right names). Howe was filtering 1963 through his own intense sense of political purpose. The question of the black writer's mission arose for Howe at what was not only a burning historical juncture for the country but a moment that for him was both promising and treacherous. To his mind, the mission of James Baldwin might have echoed his own—to make the essay an instrument of guidance for a political movement, retaining a critical edge and a temperate hope, even as Howe began to fear that his own moment was passing.

For 1963 was also the moment of the New Left—to Howe both a vindication and a menace. Students for a Democratic Society was on the move, and a group of SDS leaders, of whom I was one, were invited to meet that fall with Howe and other *Dissent* editors, only to find that the collision between our two groups was more vivid than the solidarity we both hoped for. This is not the place to review the particulars. The occasion has been amply described— Howe wrote about it twice, once in an article in the *New Republic*, then in his memoir, *A Margin of Hope;* I wrote about it myself, in *The Sixties: Years of Hope, Days of Rage;* it crops up again in recollections by Howe, Tom Hayden, and me in Joseph Dorman's documentary film *Arguing the World* and in the book of the same name that Dorman drew from his interview transcripts.[19] This encounter shows up again and again because the collision was emblematic and haunting. Suffice to say that *Dissent* welcomed SDS and just as quickly bridled at us. Howe found Tom Hayden outrageously strident, "rigid," "fanatical." Howe thought Hayden not so much naive as authoritarian and deployed against him his favorite adjective for dangerous willfulness: "He spoke with the clenched authority of a party leader."[20] Hayden, for his part, found Howe overbearing, paternalistic, high decibel—Hayden might well have used the word *clenched* himself. By the time I interviewed Howe about this encounter in 1985, he had realized that what he was objecting to in Hayden was not warmed-over Bolshevism but Howe's old nemesis, the self-made, historically innocent, thrusting transcendentalist style of Henry David Thoreau.

Considering the temperature of the moment, then, we may surmise that "Black Boys and Native Sons" represented Howe's struggle with his own duality—an attempt to group all his commitments in one place. It failed. When his politics swamped his literary sensibility, he was asking for trouble. And it came from a formidable source: Ellison. (Nicely enough, from Ralph *Waldo* Ellison.[21])The charged jarring quality of this historical moment probably helps explain Ellison's fierce rejoinder, soon followed by his rejoinder to Howe's rejoinder—all in all, possibly the most trenchant attack ever directed at Howe's criticism. In the *New Leader* Ellison lashed out:

> Why is it so often true that when critics confront the American as *Negro* they suddenly drop their advanced critical armament and revert with an air of confident superiority to quite primi-

tive modes of analysis? Why is it that sociology-oriented critics seem to rate literature so far below politics and ideology that they would rather kill a novel than modify their presumptions concerning a given reality which it seeks in its own terms to project? Finally, why is it that so many of those who would tell us the meaning of Negro life never bother to learn how varied it really is?[22]

Ellison was relentless: "Appearing suddenly in black face . . . evidently Howe feels that unrelieved suffering is the only 'real' Negro experience... . One unfamiliar with what Howe stands for would get the impression that when he looks at a Negro he sees not a human being but an abstract embodiment of living hell." Most pointedly, Ellison accused the critic of a breach of critical faculties: Howe, he wrote, seemed to have missed the irony that the narrator of *Invisible Man* spoke of his life as one of "infinite possibilities" "while living in a hole in the ground."[23] In reply, Howe protested that Ellison had got him wrong in many particulars (not, however, apropos his having missed the context of the "infinite possibilities" remark) and accused Ellison of playing to "the liberal audience." But Howe sounded uncharacteristically fastidious and defensive.

In truth, Ellison and Howe in 1963 were secret sharers. Ellison was fending off pressure from militant black writers like Baldwin. Defending his ground against younger, more "clenched" rivals,[24] Ellison gritted his teeth, ready to tangle with anyone who would presume to lecture him, like Howe, with "Olympian authority." Ellison fending off militant writers resembled Howe fending off New Left activists. They were both fighting with heirs who would wound them—and whom they would outlast.

To return to my primary theme: Having evoked such a blazing reaction when he violated his own rule against literary discussion in *Dissent,* is it any wonder that Howe would refrain from violating it again? Not only had he permitted politics to swamp literature—and thus his own critical sensibility—but he had been authoritatively chastised for it, even if he later reprinted his article more than once and on the surface seemed to think he had fought Ellison to a draw (at least). Why run the risk of more such imbroglios and embarrassments? And if he didn't trust himself to connect politics and literature in *Dissent*, why would he trust anyone else? Once badly burned, forever wary.

III

Every modern intellectual has a pet bête noir—perhaps more than one but one that stands out. George Orwell's, for example, is the obfuscating apologist for totalitarianism, hiding servility beneath a show of moral toughness, freely laying gifts at the feet of the powerful while pretending to cultic knowledge of historical inevitability. Jean-Paul Sartre's is that bastard of a bourgeois whose rigor of taste and assurance of superiority are no more than disguises for callousness. For C. Wright Mills it is the smiling courtier who rationalizes inaction, teamed up with the crackpot realist and the abstracted empiricist.

A bête noir can be useful, someone to think against—up to the tic point, when the barbarian, in the words of Cavafy's great poem (a poem of which Howe was fond, by the way), emerges as "a sort of solution" to the problem of freedom, which in a writer is the problem of what to do with the next blank page. The strongest minds probe their obsessions, wonder whether the devil is a brother under the skin; the merely compulsive repeat themselves out of sheer pleasure of habit or incapacity to do anything else. For them the beast is unchanging and unchangeable, ever and always the same—the essential bourgeois or, for that matter, Jew—and so one always knows what to say about it. One can be chained to one's bête noir, sacrificing freedom to a ideal of rectitude that becomes an excuse for intellectual laziness. When to know this has happened is hard.

It is difficult to resist the idea that a bête noir is the man or woman whom one hates with special intensity *because one has known the temptation*. I hope this does not strike the reader as cheap psychologizing. I mean it as expensive psychologizing—not only because it is useful to understand one's obsessions, but because it undermines one's self-satisfaction to discover that hated foe, corrupt, brutal, and treacherous is, after all, *mon sem-blable, mon frère.*

Irving Howe's bête noire was the man of action—an interesting choice, given that his hero was also a man of action. People may, "in the end," represent social formations—Howe was, after all, some sort of Marxist most of his life—but the end is not where people live. On the actual terrain where people live out their purposes, they may do their representing either slackly and unconsciously or forcefully and consciously. The man of action may be representative but that is not the striking thing about him. He must be outstanding. Howe was drawn to the forceful man (not so much to the forceful woman, as his feminist critics did not tire of pointing out, with the possible exception of Hardy's Tess), but he was fiercely antagonistic to the "clenched," fist-pounding, self-making type. To bask in a pool of "infinite possibilities" was delusional, but to go to the opposite pole, to "clench up," was worse. In the history of American writing—indeed, of American identity—he traced this type to Emerson's "active conquering 'self,'" though Emerson's own style was more relaxed than clenched.[25] In politics, clenching lent itself to what Howe called "radical posturing."[26] I have already noted that he found Tom Hayden "clenched," though Howe later confessed that he had been wrong to identify Hayden's style with quasi-Communist authoritarianism; Howe came to realize that what Hayden exemplified, rather, was the Emersonian temper, a home-grown ego-bound willfulness.[27] This haunting archetype was also visible in the self-inflated Jay Gatsby, who sprang, his creator, F. Scott Fitzgerald, wrote, "from his Platonic conception of himself."[28] In the arts it appeared as "clenched prometheanism" and the "inflamed" will. In modern life clenching was everywhere. You tried to break away from convention, order, responsibility, and you ended up clenched, even crippled.

Wherever it roamed, Emersonian self-reliance curdled individualism into an ideology, leading "toward a tragic sundering between democratic sentiment and individualist aggrandizement."[29] Emerson's Promethean streak metastasized in the abundantly talented but ultimately antisocial Thoreau, whose "commitment to an absolute selfhood—at its least attractive, a private utopia for anarchic curmudgeons—implies an antipathy not only to the idea of government but to the very nature and necessary inconveniences of liberal government. Ultimately derived from liberalism, the Emersonian ethos has here been driven toward an antiliberal extreme."[30] All self-creating extremes were destined for the precipice. An individual striving to tear himself free of his past was like a whole society striving to "disentangle itself from historical conditions . . . the proclaimed goal of all serious revolutions."[31] Both were giddy, both delusional, both hazardous.

In Howe's writing over the years the adjective *clenched* shows up surprisingly often; so does its cousin, *coiled*. Richard Wright's posture is one of "clenched militancy."[32] T. E. Lawrence goes through "the cycle of exertion—a moment of high excitement, a plunge into activity, then sickness, self-scrutiny, the wild desire to escape and finally a *clenched* return."[33] A few pages later Lawrence's writing gives off a sense of "teeth clenched"; he is "a figure coiled with energy and purpose."[34] Hemingway's work offered "devotion to clenched styles of survival"; his stories had a "clenched shape . . . insisting that no one can escape, moments of truth come to all of us."[35] Even as physical description, *clenched* is a mark of confinement and punishment, as, early in Howe's intellectual autobiography, he describes the apartment buildings of the East Bronx as "clenched into rows."[36]

A clenched existence is not a happy state, but exactly what Howe meant by it is not very clear. Rigidified will? The state of suffocation that D. H. Lawrence called "cramp"? The suppression of wild freedom? Whatever exactly Howe was warning against, his prolonged preoccupation suggests that he felt the need to renounce and resist a certain temptation. The longing to break loose had to be managed. What to do? (This was Freud's question, too.) From time to time personal life might unleash the impulse to break the rules. Literature could let this impulse out to play, indulge it, and, if need be, give it the rope to hang by. But politics had to operate in the key of responsibility. Even at the cost of going gray, responsible politics had to keep the anarchic streak under control—clenched. Indeed, in public debates Irving himself impressed many observers as clenched. Clenching was tragically useful.

IV

Here is another partition in Irving Howe's life and work: he wrote extensively on political novelists (Stendhal, Dostoyevsky, Conrad, Silone, and Orwell, among others), but none of his three full-length literary studies is about one of them. None of his book-length subjects wrote much about politics at all. The differences among Sherwood Anderson, William Faulkner, and Thomas Hardy are tremendous, but all wrote about worlds that are both local and densely imagined. All three cared deeply about the moral life, but none celebrated political action. To the contrary: all honored the ordinary flow of human existence.

This is perhaps to say no more than that Howe, as critic, played in more than one key. The "mania for totality" that he loathed in politics he admired in literature—in the integrity and decency of a unified character *(Tess of the D'Urbervilles)* or the unified style of narrative ferocity *(Michael Kohlhaas)*.[37] Politics, at least in the nineteenth century, can be a chance for heroism, and this is partly because the hero becomes whole by fusing with his plot, becoming an emanation of it.[38] In life the heroic moralistic will was hazardous (if fascinating, as with T. E. Lawrence), but in literature the ferocious will could electrify. Howe found "entrancing" Kleist's novella *Michael Kohlhaas,* about a character who disappears into his actions, his intensity and wholeness in the name of justice congealing into vengefulness. Kleist's relentless narrative method "permits a unity of experience which in almost every segment of our culture we know to have been lost."[39] Yet literature also did well to honor the antiheroic, antimoralistic virtues and textures of normal existence. Howe admired writers who apotheosized ordinariness, the rhythms of plain life. His son, Nicholas, tells us that Howe once considered a short book on such underestimated "poets of everyday life" as George Crabbe, George Meredith, Edwin Arlington Robinson, Thomas Hardy, and Edward Thomas, whose "restrained style and stubborn wisdom moved him."[40] About Hardy, Howe wrote: "In Hardy's refusal of moralism there is something morally exhilarating: it is, I think, a source of that subdued glow of humaneness which brightens his pages."[41] These are not the virtues of heroes, but without this "subdued glow" heroism loses its raison d'être and becomes unbridled, or "clenched." Indeed, Howe wrote in his polemic against Kate Millett: "In the history of modern intellectual life nothing has been more disastrous than this hatred of 'the usual.'"[42]

Paradoxically, his appreciation of the usual sent him back to a literary appreciation of the hero. Thus his apparently strange attraction to T. E. Lawrence. On the face of it Lawrence was a curious choice as a major figure in the writings of a socialist critic—the "centerpiece," as Howe wrote, for one of his essay collections.[43] Lawrence was a nationalist, if by proxy. But like some of Hardy's, Anderson's, and Faulkner's heroes, Lawrence was a man who acted in the name of a settled community. He was a hero in search of a people in the name of whom to act freely and consequentially. Lawrence's heroism, Howe wrote, conveyed the possibility of stamping intelligence and value upon a segment of history. To leave behind the settled life of middle-class England, which seemed to offer little but comfort and destruction; to abandon the clutter of routine by which a man can fill his days, never knowing his capacity for sacrifice or courage; to break with the assumption that life consists merely of waiting for things to happen—these were yearnings that Lawrence discovered in the Arab revolt. And these are the motifs of his conduct that made him so attractive to an age in which the capacities for heroism seemed constantly to diminish.[44]

So, too, in his late works Howe turned back, generously, to the untamed individual. He even half warmed toward Emerson while retaining his suspicion of a writer who, he thought, had so little sociability and solidarity in him. Howe wrote sympathetically of an unclenched Emerson, the Emerson who did not want to depart from society but to "recompose" it, to "animate labor by love and society . . . [to] destroy the value of many kinds of property, and replace all property within the dominion of reason and equity."[45] Emerson was noble—the transcendent, lonely, apotheosized democrat who ultimately failed "because all such projects fail."[46] If Howe could applaud Stendhal for writing "devil's manuals for men in revolt at a time when there is no possibility of revolt," he could come around to welcoming Emerson's revolt of withdrawal.[47]

Howe loved the "wild disorder" that undermined systematic structure in the novel.[48] In literature, eruptions and revelations were compatible with an affection for the everyday—Hardy's or Faulkner's, say. But such undermining belonged on the page, not in politics. In politics the prime virtue was steadiness. In the most ordinary circumstances a political organizer always had to find something useful to do. Politics, like waiting for the messiah, was, in a Yiddish punch line that Howe borrowed for the title of an essay collection, steady work. Yet late in his life Howe had come around to recognizing, with some chagrin, that politics—radical politics, anyway—required rather more excitement. In his intellectual memoir, *A Margin of Hope* (no giddy promise of breakthrough in that title), he quoted the political theorist George Kateb to the effect that the problem with social democracy was that it was *boring*. But so be it.

Politics, in other words, is intrinsically tragic. Without limits it is lethal. Respecting limits, it slides toward the tedious—which is why, by way of compensation, we require art. The sustaining style of politics affords no more than "a margin of hope." But when politics collapses into style, it overwhelms reason and becomes *bad* politics. The political equivalent of the New York intellectuals' "bravura," their "brilliance of gesture," was the New Left bravado that he roundly—somewhat viciously, somewhat prophetically—condemned in 1965 as the New Left's "new styles in 'leftism.'"[49] When style (as opposed to values, ideals, and strategy) became central to politics, it was because politics was dissolving into style and ceasing to be politics altogether—as with the grandiose deceptions of the Black Panthers and the desperado nihilism of the Weathermen.

Style masquerading as politics Irving Howe devoured in literature. It was his fascination. Even his suspicion of it deepened his fascination. Much as he was devoted to style, he strained to keep it in its place. So the partition he built up between his political and his literary life in the course of his thirty-eight years with *Dissent* was not incidental. It was not papier-mâché. It was solid—it had to be solid. But to keep it in place was—yes—steady work.

Notes

1. But around 1990 Howe told another board member, David Bromwich, that *Dissent* ought to review certain novels because of their quality and interest. Robert Stone's *A Flag for Sunrise* was an example. Such reviews did not materialize, however—I think because Irving's commitment to commissioning them was weak (personal communication, David Bromwich, September 8, 2003).
2. Irving Howe, "The New York Intellectuals," *Decline of the New* (New York: Horizon Press, 1970), pp. 240–42.
3. Brian Morton to Todd Gitlin, December 28, 2002.
4. Howe, *Politics and the Novel* (1957; reprint, New York: Avon, 1967), p. 180.
5. Howe, "History and the Novel: Variations on a Theme," in *A Critic's Notebook,* ed. Nicholas Howe (New York: Harcourt Brace Jovanovich, 1994), p. 196.
6. Ibid.
7. Scheler, epigraph to Howe, *Politics and the Novel.*
8. Howe, *Politics and the Novel,* p. 193.
9. Howe, *Celebrations and Attacks: Thirty Years of Literary and Cultural Commentary* (New York: Horizon, 1979), p. 100.
10. Ibid., p. 101.
11. Howe, "Black Boys and Native Sons," *Dissent,* Fall 1963, p. 364. Howe incorporated in his piece for *Dissent* material that originally appeared in his *Nation* piece eleven years earlier.
12. Ibid., p. 354.
13. Howe, *Thomas Hardy* (1966; reprint, New York: Collier, 1985), p. 173.
14. Howe, "Black Boys and Native Sons," p. 366.
15. Ibid., p. 367.
16. Ibid.
17. Ibid., p. 368.
18. Ibid.
19. Dorman, *Arguing the World: The New York Intellectuals in Their Own Words* (New York: Free Press, 2000), pp. 139–44.
20. Howe, "The Fleeting New Left: Historical Memory, Political Vision," *New Republic,* November 9, 1974, p. 26.
21. "While I am without doubt a Negro and a writer, I am also an American writer," Ralph Ellison, "A Rejoinder," *New Leader,* January 3, 1964, p. 16.

22. Ralph Ellison, "The World and the Jug," *New Leader*, December 9, 1963, p. 22.

23. Ibid., p. 23.

24. Curiously and, I think, erroneously, Ellison took Howe's reference to Wright's "clenched militancy" as a complimentary one (Ellison, "The World and the Jug," p. 26).

25. Howe, *The American Newness: Culture and Politics in the Age of Emerson* (Cambridge, Mass.: Harvard University Press, 1986), p. 41.

26. Ibid., p. 32.

27. In a 1985 interview with me, parts of which are quoted in Todd Gitlin, *The Sixties: Years of Hope, Days of Rage* (New York: Bantam, 1987), pp. 172–73.

28. Quoted in Howe, *The American Newness,* p. 7.

29. Ibid., p. 42.

30. Howe, *Celebrations and Attacks,* p. 247.

31. Howe, *American Newness,* p. 21.

32. Howe, "Black Boys and Native Sons," p. 360.

33. Howe, "T. E. Lawrence: The Problem of Heroism," in *A World More Attractive: A View of Modern Literature and Politics* (New York: Horizon, 1963), p. 17, emphasis added.

34. Ibid., p. 25.

35. Howe, "The Quest for Moral Style," in *A World More Attractive,* pp. 66, 70.

36. Howe, *A Margin of Hope: An Intellectual Autobiography* (New York: Harcourt Brace Jovanovich, 1982), p. 2.

37. Howe, *Politics and the Novel,* p. 53.

38. Ibid., p. 41.

39. Howe, *A Critic's Notebook,* p. 61.

40. Nicholas Howe, introduction to *A Critic's Notebook,* p. 15.

41. Irving Howe, *Thomas Hardy,* p. 167.

42. Howe, *The Critical Point* (New York: Horizon, 1973), p. 229.

43. Howe, *A World More Attractive,* p. x.

44. Ibid., p. 18.

45. Howe, *The American Newness,* p. 22, citing Emerson's "Introductory Lecture."

46. Ibid., p. 26.

47. Howe, *Politics and the Novel,* p. 35.

48. Howe, *Thomas Hardy,* p. 98.

49. Howe, "New Styles in 'Leftism,'" *Dissent,* summer 1965, reprinted in *Selected Writings, 1950–1990* (New York: Harcourt Brace Jovanovich, 1990), p. 194.

II. Two Traps and Three Values

Weak thinking on the American left is especially glaring after September 11, 2001, as I'll argue in part III, but this is hardly to say that the right has been more impressive at making the world comprehensible. For decades the right has cultivated its own types of blindness and more than that: having risen to political power, it has been in a position to make blindness the law of the land. The neoconservatives' foreign policy is largely hubris under a veneer of ideals. The antigovernment dogma of deregulation, privatization, and tax cuts exacerbates economic and social troubles. A culture war against modernity—against secularism, feminism, and racial justice—flies in the face of the West's distinctive contribution to the history of civilization, namely, the rise of individual rights and reason.

To elaborate on these claims is the work of other books. The reasons for the right-wing ascendancy are many, among them— as I argued in letter 7 of *Letters to a Young Activist* (2003)—the organizational discipline that the right cherishes and the left, at least until recently, tends to abhor. The left's institutions, in particular, unions, are weak. But my focus here is another reason for the right's ascendancy: the left's intellectual disarmament.

Some of the deficiency is institutional. Despite efforts to come from behind after the 2000 election, there remain decades' worth of shortfall in the left's cultural apparatus. In action-minded think tanks, talk radio and cable television, didactic newspapers, subsidies for writers, and so on, the right has held most of the high cards.[1] Left and liberal analyses and proposals do emerge from universities and research centers, but their circulation is usually choked off for lack of focus, imagination, and steady access to mass media—except in the cheapened forms of punditry and agitprop.

The right's masterful apparatus for purveying its messages and organizing for power is not the only reason why the left has suffered defeat after defeat in national politics since the 1960s. The left's intellectual stockpile has been badly depleted, and new ideas are more heralded than delivered. When the left has thought big, it has been clearer about *isms* to oppose—mainly imperialism and racism—than about values and policies to further. At that, it has often preferred the denunciatory mode to the analytical, mustering full-throated opposition rather than full-brained exploration. While it is probably true that many more reform ideas are dreamt of than succeed in circulating through the brain-dead media, the liberal-left conveys little sense of a whole that is more than the sum of its parts. While the right has rather successfully tarred liberals with the brush of "tax-and-spend," those thus tarred have often been unsure whether to reply "It's not so" or "It *is* so, we're proud to say." A fair generalization is that the left's expertise has been constricted in scope, showing little taste for principle and little capacity to imagine a reconstituted nation. It has been conflicted and unsteady about values. It has tended to disdain any design for foreign policy other than "U.S. out," which is no substitute for a foreign policy—and inconsistent to boot when you consider that the left wants the United States to intervene, for example, to push Israel to end its occupation of the West Bank.

All this is to say that the left has been imprisoned in the closed world of outsider politics. Instead of a vigorous quest for testable propositions that could actually culminate in reform, the academic left in particular has nourished what has come to be called "theory": a body of writing (one can scarcely say its content consists of propositions) that is, in the main, distracting, vague, self-referential, and wrong-headed. "Theory" is chiefly about itself: "thought to the second power," as Fredric Jameson defined dialectical thinking in an early, dazzling American exemplar of the new theoretical style.[2] Even when "theory" tries to reconnect from language and mind to the larger social world, language remains the preoccupation. Michel Foucault became a rock star of theory in the United States precisely because he demoted knowledge to a reflex of power, merely the denominator of the couplet "power/knowledge," yet his preoccupation was with the knowledge side, not actual social structures. His famous illustration of the power of "theory" was built on Jeremy Bentham's design of an ideal prison, the Panopticon—a model never built.[3] The "linguistic turn" in the social sciences turns out to be its own prison house, equipped with funhouse mirrors but no exit.

When convenient, "theory" lays claim to objective truth, but in fact the chief criterion by which it ascended in status was aesthetic, not empirical. Flair matters more than explanatory power. At crucial junctures "theory" consists of flourishes, intellectual performance pieces: things are said to be so because the theorist says so, and even if they are not, isn't it interesting to pretend? But the problem with "theory" goes beyond opaque writing—an often dazzling concoction of jargon, illogic, and preening. If you overcome bedazzlement at the audacity and glamour of theory and penetrate the obscurity, you find circularity and self-justification, often enough (and self-contradictorily) larded with populist sentimentality about "the people" or "forces of resistance." You see steadfast avoidance of tough questions. Despite the selective use of the still-prestigious rhetoric of science, the world of "theory" makes only tangential contact with the social reality that it disdains. Politically, it is useless. It amounts to secession from the world where most people live.

Yet the audacious adepts of "theory" constitute themselves the equivalent of a vanguard party—laying out propositions to be admired for their audacity rather than their truth, defending themselves when necessary as victims of stodgy and parochial old-think, priding themselves on their cosmopolitan majesty. "Theory" dresses critical thought in a language that, for all its impenetrability, certifies that intellectuals are central and indispensable to the ideological and political future. The far right might be firmly in charge of Washington, but Foucault (and his rivals) rules the seminars. At a time of political rollback, intellectual flights feel like righteous and thrilling consolations.

Masters of "theory," left to themselves, could choose among three ways of understanding their political role. They could choose the more-or-less Leninist route, flattering themselves that they are in the process of reaching correct formulations and hence (eventually) bringing true consciousness to benighted souls who suffer from its absence. They could choose the populist path, getting themselves off the political hook in the here and now by theorizing that potent forces will some day, willy-nilly, gather to upend the system. Or they could reconcile themselves to Frankfurt-style futilitarianism, conceding that history has run into a cul-de-sac and making do nevertheless. In any event, practitioners of "theory" could carry on with their lives, practicing politics by publishing without perishing, indeed, without having to set foot outside the precincts of the academy. As the revolutionary tide has gone out, a vanguard marooned without a rearguard has made the university into an asylum. As many founders and masters of "theory" pass from the scene, the genre has calcified, lost much of its verve, but in the academy verve is no prerequisite for institutional weight, and so the preoccupation and the style go on and on.

In *The Twilight of Common Dreams: Why America Is Wracked by Culture Wars* (1995), I argued against one of the fixations of "theory": the strong form of identity politics, the aggrandizement of multiculturalism, which overstresses the fixity of segmented "identity" and the boundaries between social segments. There is no point to repeating those arguments here. Nearly a decade after writing that book, I would make virtually the same case about the intellectual slovenliness and political inconsequence (or worse) that runs rife with the hypertrophy of identity politics. My sense, though, is that in the interim, identity politics has sunk into a rut of normality. Hard-core exponents of identity politics have probably dwindled and certainly softened. Some die-hard opponents have also backed off, observing that as "identity" has been institutionalized in academic programs, it has lost a good deal of its bite. Today, at least in the vanguard elite institutions, "hybridity" is more honored than the fervent cultivation of difference. Diversity is a goal that majorities or near-majorities can subscribe to. As Nathan Glazer, once one of the more cogent critics of affirmative action, put it in the title of his 1997 book, we are all multiculturalists now—at least rhetorically.

In the second part of this book, then, I address two related themes in the academic left's thinking since the mid-1970s: the overall postmodernist mood, especially as manifest in "theory," and the antipolitical populism of cultural studies. These tendencies were among the conditions for an intellectual default. Then I turn to conflicts among values—media, citizenship, and education—hoping to sketch where we might look for help in the realm of the higher learning.

Notes

1. On the right's investment in think tanks, college newspapers, right-wing attack media, and other nodes in a vast publicity grid, see chap. 6 of my *The Twilight of Common Dreams: Why American Is Wracked by Culture Wars* (New York: Metropolitan, 1995), and John Micklethwait and Adrian Wooldridge, *The Right Nation: Conservative Power in America* (New York: Penguin, 2004), chap. 6. On right-wing domination of talk television and wholly owned newspapers, see Eric Alterman, *Sound and Fury: The Making of the Punditocracy,* paperback ed. (Ithaca, N.Y.: Cornell University Press, 2000), and Alterman, *What Liberal Media? The Truth About Bias and the News* (New York: Basic, 2003). On right-wing media generally see David Brock, *Blinded by the Right: The Conscience of an Ex-conservative* (New York: Crown, 2002), and Brock, *The Republican Noise Machine: Right-Wing Media and How It Corrupts Democracy* (New York: Random House, 2004).

2. Jameson, *Marxism and Form: Twentieth-century Dialectical Theories of Literature* (Princeton, N.J.: Princeton University Press, 1972), pp. 372ff.

3. Foucault, *Discipline and Punish: The Birth of the Prison* (New York: Pantheon, 1977), pp. 200ff.

4

The Postmodernist Mood

What was postmodernism? Commentators pro, con, serious, fey, academic, and even accessible seem agreed that something postmodern happened in the last generation or two, even if we were virtually all Mr. Jones, who didn't know what it was. The volume and pitch of the commentary implied that something about this postmodern something *mattered*. Something, it seemed, had happened in the world. It would be cute but glib and shortsighted to dismiss the talk as so much time-serving space filling, the shoring up of positions for the sake of amassing theoretical property, or propriety, or priority. There was anxiety at work and at play. I think it is reasonable, or at least interesting, to assume that the anxiety that surfaced in the course of the discussion was called for.

Though eventually journalists began to use *postmodernist* to label anything newfangled, in knowing discourse the term—*pomo,* for short—mainly referred to a certain constellation of styles and tones in culture: pastiche; blankness; a sense of exhaustion; a mixture of levels, forms, styles; a relish for copies and repetition; a knowingness that rejects authenticity and dissolves commitment into irony; acute self-consciousness about the formal, constructed nature of language, art, and other symbolic transactions; pleasure in the play of surfaces; a rejection of big ideas ("metanarratives"). In the pastures of theory postmodernism ran parallel to its swath through the arts, featuring the belief that discourse was central to the human situation and that indeterminacy was central to discourse, and rejecting the possibility or virtue of reason. Pomo was Michael Graves's Portland Building and Philip Johnson's AT&T (later renamed for SONY when the building changed hands—an amusing pomo move, come to think of it); it was photorealism, conceptual art (however blurry the concepts), David Hockney, Robert Rauschenberg's silk screens, Andy Warhol's multiple-image paintings and Brillo boxes, Larry Rivers's erasures and pseudopageantry; Sherrie Levine's photographs of "classic" photographs and Richard Prince's photographs of ads; it was Disneyland, Las Vegas, suburban strips, shopping malls, mirror glass facades; it was bricolage fashion; it was news commentary cluing us in to the imaging-making and positioning strategies of the candidates; it was William Burroughs, Italo Calvino, Jorge Luis Borges, Donald Barthelme, Monty Python, Don DeLillo, the Kronos Quartet, David Letterman, Paul Auster; it was Michel Foucault, Jacques Derrida, Jacques Lacan, Jean Baudrillard. What was at stake in the debate—and thus the root of the general anxiety—went beyond style: it was really a question of what disposition toward public life was going to prevail.

Postmodernism in the arts corresponded to postmodernism in life, as sketched by the French theorist Jean-François Lyotard: "One listens to reggae, watches a western, eats McDonald's food for lunch and local cuisine for dinner, wears Paris perfume in Tokyo, and 'retro' clothes in Hong Kong."[1] The entire phenomenon called postmodernism is best understood as a way of apprehending and experiencing the world and our place, or placelessness, in it. (Just whose place or placelessness is at issue is a question to which I shall return.) So controversies about postmodernism were in no small part discussions about how to live, feel, think in a specific world, our own: a world of what David Harvey called "space-time compression," a world both alluring and nerve-racking, a world no longer swayed by the hopes and desperate innocence of the sixties, a world unimpressed by the affirmative futurology of Marxism.

The discussion of postmodernism was, among other things, a deflected and displaced discussion of the contours of political thought—in the largest sense—during the seventies and eighties. Postmodernism claimed to be a transcendence of history, but its spirit was embedded—where else?—in history. Postmodernism was, in this sense, an extended deferral, an emptiness defined not by what it was but by what it followed. The very term had trouble establishing either the force or the originality of the concept. Why did this emptiness come to pass?

Things must be made to look crystalline for a moment before complications set in. Here is the first approximation of a grid for distinguishing among premodernist realism, modernism, and postmodernism. These are rough versions of ideal types, mind you, not adequate descriptions. They are not necessarily ideal types of the work "itself" but, rather, of the work as understood and judged by some consensus of artists, critics, and audiences.

The premodernist work aspired to a unity of vision. It cherished continuity, speaking with a single narrative voice or addressing a single visual center. It honored sequence and causality in time or space. Through the consecutive, the linear, it claimed to represent reality. It might contain a critique of the established order, in the name of the obstructed ambitions of individuals, or it might uphold individuals as the embodiments of society at its best. In either event, individuals mattered. The work observed, highlighted, rendered judgments, and exuded passions in their names. Standing apart from reality, the work aspired to an order of beauty, which, in a sense, judged reality. Lyrical forms, heightened speech, rhythm and rhyme, Renaissance perspective, and compositional axioms went to work in the interests of the sublime. Finally, the work might borrow stories and tunes from popular materials but it held itself (and was held by its audience) above its origins; high culture held the line against the popular.

The modernist work might aspire to unity, but it was a unity under construction, assembled from fragments or shocks or juxtapositions. It shifted abruptly among a multiplicity of voices, perspectives, materials. Continuity was disrupted, and enthusiastically: it was as if the work was punctuated with exclamation marks. The orders of conventional reality—inside versus outside, subject versus object, self versus other—were called into question. So were the orders of art: poetry versus prose, painting versus sculpture, representation versus reality. The work was apocalyptic, often fused with a longing for some long-gone organic whole sometimes identified with a fascist or revolutionary present or future. Usually, though, the protagonist was not so much opposed to as estranged from or ambivalent toward the prevailing order. The work composed beauty out of discord. Aiming to bring into sharp relief the line between art and life, modernism appropriated selected shards of popular culture and quoted from them.

In the postmodernist sensibility the search for unity was apparently abandoned altogether. Instead we had textuality, a cultivation of surfaces endlessly referring to, ricocheting from, reverberating onto, other surfaces. The work called attention to its constructedness; it interrupted itself. Instead of a single center, there was cultural recombination. Anything could be juxtaposed to anything else. Everything took place in the present, "here," that is, nowhere in particular. The authoritative voice dissolved, to be replaced by deadpan mockery or bemusement. The work labored under no illusions: we are all deliberately pretending here, get the point? There was a premium on copies; everything has been done. Shock, now routine, was greeted with the glazed stare or smirk of the absolute ironist. The implied subject was unstable, even decomposed; it was finally nothing more than a crosshatch of discourses. Where there was once passion or ambivalence, there was now a collapse of feeling, a blankness. Beauty, deprived of its power of criticism in an age of packaging, was irrelevant or distracting. Genres were spliced; so were cultural gradations. "High culture" didn't so much quote from popular culture as blur into it.

All master styles aim to remake the history that precedes them, just as T. S. Eliot said individual talents reorder tradition. In one sense, then, postmodernism remade the relation between premodernism and modernism. In the light of postmodern disdain for representational conventions, the continuity between the preceding stages came to seem more striking than the chasm dividing them. If the phenomenon were more clearly demarcated from its predecessor, it might have been able to stand, semantically, on its own feet. Instead, *post*modernism defined the present cultural space as a sequel, in relation to what it no longer was.

So what was new? It has been argued, with considerable force, that the lineaments of postmodernism are already present in one or another version of modernism, that postmodernism was simply the current incarnation, or phase, in a still-unfolding modernism. Roger Shattuck made the point that cubism, futurism, and artistic spiritualists like Kandinsky "shared one compositional principle: the juxtaposition of states of mind, of different times and places, of different points of view."[2] Collage, montage: these were the essence of modernism high and low. Then what was so special about (1) Philip Johnson's AT&T building, with its Chippendale pediment on high and quasi-classical columns below; (2) the Australian Circus Oz, which combined jugglers who commented on their juggling and cracked political jokes along with (its list) "Aboriginal influences, vaudeville, Chinese acrobats, Japanese martial arts, firemen's balances, Indonesian instruments and rhythms, video, Middle eastern tunes, B-grade detective movies, modern dance, Irish jigs, and the ubiquitous present of corporate marketing"; (3) the student who walked into my office dressed in green jersey, orange skirt, and black tights?

Put it this way: modernism shredded unity and postmodernism scampered among the shreds. Modernism tore asunder what postmodernism mixed in and about. Modernism's multiplication of perspective led to postmodernism's utter dispersion of voices; modernist collage made possible postmodernist genre splicing. The point of pomo was not only juxtaposition but attitude. Postmodern juxtaposition had a deliberate self-consciousness. The point was to skate on the edge dividing irony from dismay or endorsement. Picasso, Boccioni, Tatlin, Pound, Joyce, Woolf in their various ways thundered and hungered. Their work was radiant with passion and self-confidence. Postmodernists, by contrast, were blasé, bemused, or exhausted: they'd seen it all.

I have been pushing postmodernism into the past, but its recombinatory thrust, its blankness, its self-referential irony, and its play of surfaces are still very much with us. Architecture's pastiches may have passed into shtick, but what was interesting was not a single set of architectural tropes but postmodernism as what Raymond Williams called a "structure of feeling"—an interlocking cultural complex combining "characteristic elements of impulse, restraint, and tone"—that colored the common experience of a society.[3] In this flickering half-light postmodernism was significant because its amalgam of spirits penetrated architecture, fiction, painting, poetry, planning, performance, music, television, and many other domains. It was one wing, at least, of the zeitgeist.

Where did postmodernism come from? We can distinguish five approaches to an answer. They are not necessarily incompatible. To the contrary: several forces converged to produce the postmodernist moment.

The first is the bleak Marxist account sketched by Fredric Jameson and David Harvey.[4] The postmodernist spirit, with its superseding of the problem of authenticity, belonged to, was coupled to, corresponded with, expressed—the relation was not altogether clear—the culture of multinational capitalism, in which capital, that infinitely transferable abstraction, abolished particularity as such along with the coherent self in whom history, depth, and subjectivity once united. The universal exchange value overcame authentic use value. The characteristic machine of the postmodern period is the computer, which enthrones (or fetishizes) the fragment, the "bit," and in the process places a premium on process and reproduction that is aped in postmodernist art. Surfaces meet surfaces in these postmodern forms because a new human nature—a human second nature—formed to feel at home in a homeless world political economy.

Postmodernists ransacked history for shards because there really was no here here. In fact and not just in art or in theory, the permanent revolution that is capitalism shattered historical continuity. Uprooted juxtaposition is how people live: not only displaced peasants cast into the megalopolis, where decontextualized images proliferate, but also viewers confronted with the interruptions of American television as well as financial honchos shifting bits of information and blips of capital around the world at will and high speed. Art expresses this abstract unity and vast weightless indifference through its blank repetitions (think of Warhol or Philip Glass), its exhausted antiromance, its I've-seen-it-all, striving, at best, for a kind of all-embracing surface.

A second stab at explanation called attention to our political rather than strictly economic moment. In this light the crucial location of the postmodern was *after the 1960s*. The postmodern was an aftermath, or a waiting game, because that is what we were living in: a prolonged cultural moment that was oddly weightless, shadowed by incomplete revolts, haunted by absences—a counterreformation beating against an unfinished, indeed barely begun, reformation. From this point of view postmodernism rejected historical continuity and took up residence somewhere beyond it because history *was* ruptured: by the bomb-fueled vision of a possible material end of history; by Vietnam, by drugs, by youth revolts, by women's and gay movements; in general, by the erosion of that false and devastating universality embodied in the trinity of Father, Corporation, and State.

Faith in progress under the sway of that trinity had underlain the assumption that the world displays (at least in the end) historical order and moral clarity. But cultural contradiction burst open the premises of the old cultural complex. The cultural upwellings and wildness of the sixties kicked the props out from under a teetering moral and intellectual structure, but the new house was not built. Postmodernism dispensed with moorings, then, because old certitudes actually crumbled. It strained to make the most of seriality, inauthenticity, and endless recirculation in the collective image warehouse because so much of reality *was* serial, inauthentic, and recirculated.

From this point of view postmodernism was blank because it wanted to have its commodification and eat it. That is, it knew that the cultural industry would tailor virtually any cultural goods for the sake of sales; it also wanted to display its knowingness, thereby demonstrating how superior it was to the trash market. Choose one: the resulting ironic spiral either mocked the game by playing it or played it by mocking it.

A third approach to explaining postmodernism was a refinement of the second: an argument not about history in general but about a specific generation and class. In a generational light postmodernism appeared as an outlook for Yuppies—urban, professional products of the late baby boom, born in the fifties and early sixties. Theirs was an experience of aftermath, privatization, and weightlessness. They could remember political commitment but were not animated by it—more, they suspected it; it led to trouble. They could not remember a time before television, suburbs, and shopping malls. (Indeed, the critic Cecelia Tichi argued that the blank-toned fiction of Ann Beattie, Bret Easton Ellis, Bobbie Ann Mason, and Tama Janowitz, among others, was the anesthetized expression of a television-saturated generation.[5]) They were accustomed, therefore, to rapid cuts, discontinuities, breaches of attention, culture to be indulged and disdained at the same time. They grew up taking drugs, taking them for granted, but did not associate them with spirituality or the hunger for transcendence. Knowing indifference was their "structure of feeling"—thus a taste for sarcasm, snarkiness, and cultural bricolage. They were disabused of authority, but the fusion of passion and politics rubbed them the wrong way. Their idea of government was shadowed by Vietnam and Watergate. *Their* television ran from *Saturday Night Live* and MTV through *Comedy Central*. Their mores leaned toward the libertarian and, at least until the AIDS terror, the libertine. They liked the idea of the free market as long as it promised them an endless accumulation of crafted goods, as in the (half-joking?) bumper sticker: "He Who Dies with the Most Toys Wins." The idea of public life—whether party participation or military intervention—filled them with weariness; the adventures that mattered to them were adventures of private life. But they were not in any conventional sense "right-wing": They floated beyond belief.

The aggrandizement of theory was class bound, though not only in the obvious sense. In France a mandarin class of intellectuals has a history going back to the Sorbonne of the fourteenth century and St. Thomas Aquinas. Leninism adapted the European mandarinate—slow to develop in Russia—into the idea of a vanguard class.[6] In the United States after the sixties Leninism survived in form as it withered in content. The clerisy would become the congregation. Jargon was a prerequisite for insight. If discourse was central to power, then the exposure and transformation of discourse was the left's central task, and academics would become indispensable. The university would become more than a comfort zone for left-wing intellectuals. (Irving Howe said that Marxism went to the university to die in comfort.) The university would become the main battlefield in the struggle for power. The struggle for tenure would be more than a parody of class struggle: it would be Gramsci's dream, a mobilization of organic intellectuals. Tenure produced illusions of power, a surrogate for politics. Defeated in Washington, you could march on the English Department. Washington was, after all, Washington, with its victorious conservatives and clueless liberals; what better did you expect?

The immense scale of American universities takes us into a fourth approach to explaining the growth of postmodernism, which starts from the observation that postmodernism was specifically, though not exclusively, American. Postmodernism was born in the U.S.A. because juxtaposition was one of the things that Americans do best. It was one of the defining currents of U.S. culture, especially with Emancipation and the rise of immigration in the latter part of the nineteenth century. (The other principal current is the opposite: assimilation into standard styles or myths. But this penchant is not exclusively American.) Juxtaposition was the Strip, the mall, the Galleria, Las Vegas, Times Square; it was the marketplace jamboree, the divinely grotesque disorder, amazing diversity striving for reconciliation and resisting it, the ethereal and ungrounded radiance of signs, the shimmer of the evanescent, the good-times beat of the tall tale meant to be simultaneously disbelieved and appreciated; it was vulgarized pluralism; it was the cultural logic of laissez-faire and more—an elbows-out, noisy, jostling version of something that could pass as democracy.

We are, central myths, homogenizations, and oligopolies notwithstanding, an immigrant culture, less melting pot than grab bag, perennially replenished by aliens. As long ago as 1916 Randolph Bourne wrote that "there is no distinctively American culture. It is apparently our lot rather to be a federation of cultures."7 Hollywood and the radio and television networks flattened the culture, but Bourne's vision retained life. The postmodernist, from this point of view, hitched high art to the raucous disrespectful quality that accompanied American popular culture from its beginnings. And indeed, the essential contribution of postmodernist art was that it obliterated the line—or the brow—separating the high from the low. What could be more American?

To lurch, in properly postmodern style, to the domain of high theory: The forms of representation displayed in postmodernist art rhymed or dovetailed with—extended? extenuated? corresponded to?—a crisis of bottomlessness that ran throughout poststructuralist theory. Among the practitioners of artistic postmodernism were a generation schooled in poststructuralist theory: variously, Foucault, Baudrillard, Lacan, Derrida.

All theoretical maps have empty spaces; there are things they cannot disclose, even acknowledge. Why should it be any less so for poststructuralists? I think of a graduate student I once met in Montreal. She presented herself as a committed feminist working the deconstructionist beat. She was partial to the notion that the world "is"—in quotation marks—everything that is agreed to be the case. The category of "lived experience" was, from this point of view, an atavistic concealment; what one "lived" was "constituted by" a discourse that had no more—or less—standing than any other system of discourse. I asked her if she wasn't troubled because she rooted her politics in her experience as a woman, yet from the poststructuralist point of view her emotions were to be forbidden any primacy. Yes, she admitted, it chagrined her. As a feminist she was unwilling to make her commitments dissolve into ungrounded discourse. Yet as a theorist she was compelled to explode the very ground on which she stood as a political person—the very ground that had brought her to discourse theories in the first place.

This self-exploding quality was the fundamental anomaly for poststructural theories. One was drawn to politics out of a complex of understandings and moral feelings, which crystallized into an Archimedean point for one's intellectual project. Then one turned to negative methods: the language of unmasking. Ideology, one came to understand, froze privilege and encased it in a spurious idea of the natural. Now one set out to thaw the world, to show how the "natural" was situated and partial. Discourse, one discovered, is a means of domination. Top dogs name things. Bottom dogs collaborate with top dogs when they take for granted their language and their definition of the situation.

This made sense—as far as it went. Yet discourse theories could not account for the impulse that launched the politics in the first place. Indeed, they held that such impulses should not be taken at face value. There *was* no human experience—at least none that deserved privileged treatment. Reality was discourse all the way down—analogous to postmodernism's endless play of surfaces. (David Hockney: "Surface is illusion but so is depth.") At the extremity poststructuralists were amused to flirt with the notion that not only social but natural reality was nothing more than a social—that is, ultimately, a linguistic—construction. In any event, most structuralist critics agreed that the concept of "literature," say, "assumes that something recognizable as human experience or human nature exists, aside from any form of words and from any form of society, and that this experience is put into words by an author"—thus Diane Macdonell, as if the idea that there is "human experience" were as dismissible as the idea that there is "human nature."[8] But then the ideal of a way of thinking that liberates was upended. What constituted liberation anyway, and who was entitled to say?

The impulse toward this sort of unmasking was certainly political: it stemmed from a desire to undo the hold of one system of knowledge/language/power over another. It followed from the sixties' revelations that various systems of knowledge were fundamentally implicated in injustice and violence—whether racist or sexist exclusions from literary canons or the language and science of militarism and imperial justification. But the poststructuralist move in theory flushed the Archimedean point away with the sewage of discourse.

If there was one theorist whose work seemed, at first, to be animated by the promise of the postmodern, it was Michel Foucault. Foucault's popularity in the United States stemmed in good measure from the flair with which he engaged "the politics of the personal" in a succession of tour de force studies documenting the ways in which institutions (psychiatry, medicine, prisons, sexuality) were encrustations of power and cultural assumptions. But perhaps something in his popularity suggested a radicalism of gesture more than action. Foucault's work was interrupted by his untimely death. But the last phase to reverberate throughout the Anglo-American world, the phase that culminated in volume I of *The History of Sexuality*, outlined a world of power that not only instigated resistance but required it, channeled it, and turned its energy back upon it. Power was everywhere, the tactics of "micropower" constantly "deployed" (to use the military language Foucault was partial to) against other tactics—apparently without a basis for solidarity or a strong reason to support resistance against power. Against Enlightenment ideas of universal rationality and normality, said to have justified the suppression of those found wanting in rationality and normality, Foucault enshrined respect for the principle of human diversity. But as he collapsed differences between structures of power, he neglected something essential. The liberal state was just another state, so there was no reason to prefer it to the authoritarian brand.

As Foucault said to a group of Berkeley faculty in November 1983, "There is no universal criteri[on] which permits [us] to say, This category of power relations [is] bad and those are good"—although Foucault the person had no trouble taking political positions. Why support some resistances and not others? He could or would not say. As we pressed him to articulate the ground of his positions, he took refuge in exasperated modesty—there was no general principle at stake and no substantial lacuna in his system. ("I know you support Solidarity against [the Communist Party chief Wojciech] Jaruzelski," I said to him. "But on what grounds?" "Why do you ask *me* this question?" he said indignantly. "Why don't you ask [another colleague present]?") This indignation at the very act of posing a question was nihilistic hauteur. How could there be an ethical basis for politics? How dare you ask?

This is not the place to hazard a solution to the formidable conundrum: how to elaborate a political point of view that would transcend anything-goes relativism without taking refuge in an artificial, abstract universalism? But one direction to look is toward an overarching concept of a politics of limits. Simply, there must be limits to what human beings can be permitted to do with their powers. The atrocities to which our species is prone can be understood as violations of limits. The essence of a politics must be rooted in three protections: The ecological: the earth and human life must be protected against the nuclear bomb, global warming, and other manmade depredations; the pluralist: the social group must be protected against domination by other social groups; the libertarian: the individual must be protected against domination by collectives. A politics of limits would be at once radical and conservative—it would conserve. It would respect horizontal social relations—multiplicity over hierarchy, coexistence over usurpation, difference over deference: finally, disorderly life in its flux against orderly death in its finality. The democratic vital edge of the postmodern—the love of difference and flux and the exuberantly unfinished—would infuse the spirit of politics, as it deserves to. Needless to say, this way of putting the matter leaves many questions unsettled, most grievously, what happens when there are conflicts and internal fissures among these objectives? What kind of authority, what kind of difference, is legitimate? Respect for uncertainties is of the essence. This is the properly postmodern note on which I suspend the discussion for now.

Might there be a variant of postmodernism—hot, not cool—in which pluralist exuberance and critical intelligence reinforce each other? Consider Dennis Potter's 1986 *The Singing Detective*, for example. Here was postmodernism with a heart—postmodernist techniques placed at the service of modernist transcendence. Here was jubilant disrespect for the boundaries that were supposed to segregate culture castes. But disrespect of this sort did not imply a leveling down, profaning the holy precincts of high culture. Where fey, blasé postmodernism skated along the edge, cheerfully or cheerlessly leaving doubt whether it was to be taken as critical or affirmative, Potter's exuberant drama, for all its artful playfulness, respected narrative flow and honored the force of character in the form of Michael Gambon's Philip Marlow, whose imagination generated the many fictional and remembered sequences. The integrity of Marlow's passions distinguished *The Singing Detective* from the sort of postmodernist hodgepodge that decomposes the world rather than composing a unity. Ironies served—or masked—desires, but desires *mattered*.

Cool postmodernism was an art of erosion. Make the most of stagnation, it said. Give up gracefully. That was its defining break from modernism, which was, whatever its subversive practices, a series of declarations of faith, albeit nervous ones—suprematism's future, Joyce's present, Eliot's unsurpassable past. Postmodernism, living off borrowed materials, lacked the resources for continuing self-renewal. It was a pale shadow—nothing but aftermath. A car with a dead battery can run off its generator only so long. Exhaustion is exhausting. But if deep currents have long been at work to generate our cultural anesthesia, then postmodernism is not going to vanish automatically. It will wear away in one spot while it hangs on in another—even if as no more than a set of stylistic fillips. Some of its gestures will outlast its spirit. It will attract epigones and endure, for a while, by default.

How does a culture renew itself? Not easily. At the least, artists—and theorists—would have to do something else. They would have to weary of weariness. They would have to cease being stenographers of the surfaces. They would have to decide not to coast down the currents of least resistance.

Notes

1. Jean-François Lyotard, *The Postmodern Condition: A Report on Knowledge.* (Manchester, U.K.: Manchester University Press, 1984), p. 76.
2. Roger Shattuck, *The Innocent Eye: On Modern Literature and the Arts* (New York: Farrar Straus and Giroux, 1984). See especially the chapter "Meyer Schapiro's Master Class," pp. 292–308.
3. Raymond Williams, *Marxism and Literature* (Oxford: Oxford University Press, 1977), p. 132.
4. Fredric Jameson, *Postmodernism, or, The Cultural Logic of Late Capitalism* (Durham, N.C.: Duke University Press, 1991); David Harvey, *The Condition of Postmodernity: An Enquiry into the Origins of Cultural Change* (London: Blackwell, 1990).
5. Cecelia Tichi, *Electronic Hearth: Creating an American Television Culture* (New York: Oxford University Press, 1991), pp. 219–21. About Mason, Tichi writes (p. 221): "Mason is *within* the TV environment and presumes that *her* reader is also there."
6. For these observations on the theory class I am indebted to Marshall Berman.
7. Randolph Bourne, "Trans-National America," *Atlantic Monthly,* July 1916, pp. 86–97.
8. Diane Macdonell, *Theories of Discourse: An Introduction* (New York: Blackwell, 1986), p. 5.

5

The Antipolitical Populism of Cultural Studies

Perhaps it's not surprising that academic fields tend to be cavalier, or embarrassed, about their own origins. A surplus of self-scrutiny might undermine the confidence with which a field goes about its business—except perhaps for philosophy when it's in a rollicking mood. A sociology of sociology, a history of history—by and large, these flower only when flowers are going to seed.

During its period of giddy expansion, cultural studies proved no exception to this rule. Yet a moment's reflection should assure us that cultural studies did not spring full blown from its object of study, culture. It has a history. Cultural studies arose at a moment that, like all others, had political, economic, social, and cultural dimensions. It survived and ballooned into a different moment. The relation between ideas and their settings is not one to be settled too easily. Still, students of cultural studies should not be surprised to discover that cultural studies is susceptible to analysis as an object of cultural study. For the field aggressively disbelieves in unmoved movers. This intellectual movement sees culture as a set of values and practices undertaken by particular people who live particular lives in particular settings and try to make sense of them, to express particular sentiments, solve particular problems, and reach particular goals. Then why should cultural studies refuse to see itself through the same lens? Cultural studies is itself a sort of culture performed by people who live particular lives in particular settings, trying to solve, or surpass, or transform particular problems.

I do not wish to dwell on problems of definition, whose te-
dium is matched only by inconclusiveness and circularity. The
interminable examination of what exactly constitutes cultural
studies—or its subject, culture—is itself part of the problem that
I seek to diagnose. Rather, I hope to slip (if not cut) the Gordian
knot with the simple statement that cultural studies is the activity
practiced by people who say that they are doing cultural studies.

Stanley Aronowitz observed in 1990 that "cultural studies is
a social movement."[1] If this was meant as a recommendation, I
take it to be self-serving and tautological. But as a statement of
fact, it was accurate. Something more was going on in cultural
studies than the pursuit of the ordinary academic rewards by
young and no-longer-so-young academics. Cultural studies was
booming throughout the English-speaking world. Energy was
at work, though the élan seems to be flagging at the moment.
Evidently—or so cultural studies would tell us—cultural studies
is a form of intellectual life that answers to passions and hopes
imported into its precincts from outside. As a social movement
cultural studies may not matter much beyond the precincts of the
academy, the art world, and affiliated institutions, but it certainly
responds to the energies of social and cultural movements—and
their eclipse.

In part, the growth of cultural studies derives from the growth
of its object of attention: popular culture, and its booming place
in life, especially from the 1960s on. Measure the significance
of popular culture in units of time (the average American watches television for more than four hours a day, and the citizens
of most other developed societies are not far behind) or in the
emotional loyalty of its audiences or in economic value, and the
point is evident. No economic determinism is needed to sustain
the observation that one necessary condition for the growth of
the commercial youth market was the economic boom that followed World War II and hence the growth in disposable income
among the young in the more privileged countries. Not only did
the market in popular culture grow in scale, but the young came
to define themselves by their taste, especially in popular music.
They related not only to the music but *through* the music. Popular
culture was tantamount to social membership. In part, too, the

bulking up of popular culture and celebrity stemmed from the declining grip of the institutions that traditionally imparted identity to the young: occupation, class, religion. The "other-directed" character first described by David Riesman, with the young taking their cues of membership and morality from the mass media and peer groups, has for more half a century been entrenched as the normal Western type.[2]

And popular culture has boomed outside the world of the young, too. One need not endorse the misleading slogan that we live in an "information society" to recognize that electronics and telecommunications are central to the industrial economies and, indeed, beyond economies, the very structure and texture of social and inner life overall. The transfer of images, sounds, and stories is a core feature in so-called advanced nations, not least the United States. I have tried to trace this development elsewhere and will spare the reader a recapitulation here.[3]

Politics, too, seems inconceivable outside the flows and eddies, the pumping stations and drains of industrialized culture. The intersections of popular culture and politics are so frequent, the interconnections so dense, as to spawn the exaggerated claim that the two domains have collapsed into each other. Politicians become stars and stars become politicians—Ronald Reagan, Arnold Schwarzenegger. At the margins, too, consider the U.S. counterculture: before it was a market, it was a marker of collective identity. Loved by its partisans, loathed by its enemies, popular culture in the 1960s became a fulcrum of political debate. Questions of sexuality, abortion, drugs, multiculturalism became central in political debate, and the conflicts became normalized as "culture wars."

In the 1970s the new cultural tendencies fought for legitimacy as academic subjects. The premise of the insurgent style of thought was that human beings actively and collectively make sense of their world. Historians of "mentalité" and anthropologists of culture were already staking out the territory that cultural studies would claim as its own. "History from the bottom up" thrived—social history, especially the study of historically subordinated women, African Americans, workers, and the colonized. E. P. Thompson taught that classes were made, not born.[4] For their part anthropologists brought ethnographic methods to bear on cultural life in their "home countries." Insurgent sociologists were turning away from the dismissive "collective behavior" diagnosis of social movements as, in effect, neurotic symptoms and taking seriously the professed intentions of activists, presuming them to be not only explicable but arguably rational. The early cultural studies group at Birmingham employed methods from all three fields to investigate the social history of the present—of working-class and dissident youth populations, television personages, and viewers, among others.[5] Popular cultural activity was, for all these researchers, *activity*—not the absence of something (civilization, literature, politics) but the presence of a form of engagement in the here and now. To these projects in the social sciences were added, crucially, the postmodernist turn in philosophy and "theory"—the rejection of hierarchies of value; the devaluation of "center" in favor of "periphery"; the emphasis on the active production (or "construction") of meaning; the search for "local knowledges" as opposed to truth; the insistence on self-challenging reflexivity.

The tenor of cultural studies was set, crucially, by the political circumstances of its first waves. The founding generation was deeply involved with the British New Left. Two of its founding elders, Richard Hoggart and Raymond Williams, derived from the industrial working class, and so did many of their students. Others came from the once-colonized periphery (the Jamaican immigrant Stuart Hall) and/or were women and/or gays and lesbians. They were frequently the first members of their families at the university. Designated meritocratically for the replenishment of elites, they encountered condescension alongside encouragement. Especially in Britain, they encountered programs in literary studies that had little place for the culture that these students—let alone their families—actually lived. They did not see why they should have to check their form of life at the gates. Reverence for cultural authority was not their generational spirit. They had grown up in a youth culture of enormous ambitions and, let it be said, achievements. By the late 1960s they were imbibing a youth culture itself saturated by syncretic, high-cultural masterworks of modernism—the Beatles, Bob Dylan, and so on.

They may have been taught to revere Beethoven but equally came to revere Chuck Berry, telling him to roll over and tell Tchaikovsky the news. Into the universities they carried not only their cultural points of reference but a certain texture of popular-culture experience. If reading, study sessions, rallies, and lovemaking took place against a background of rock music, they wanted to know, why shouldn't the academy also pay heed?

They were saturated with popular culture at a time when radical commitments were tinged with poignancy. In the United States in the early to mid-1970s, many veterans of the American student movement found themselves at an impasse. In the late 1960s, riding the wave of the student movement, they had committed themselves to a revolutionary breakthrough in the politics of the Western world. As the tide went out, they now found themselves beached. Insofar as they had overrated the radical potential of the young or of students as such, yet believed in a radical transformation of social life, they sought to compensate for the error by seeking out surrogate proletariats among other social groups. Marxist traditionalists found hope in a redefinition, if not revival, of a unitary "working class"—a hope that events failed to reward. Theorists of a "new working class" were quickly outdistanced by theorists and advocates of a—or "the"—third world revolution, with the majority of humanity cast in the role of world proletariat.

The radical upsurge of the late 1960s culminated in a variety of separate insurgencies but also in anticlimax and undertow. In Britain, Labour, union, feminist, and antiracist momentum continued through the 1970s, though the visible manifestations masked the fact that they had become the property of a minority—which became clear with the election of Margaret Thatcher in 1979. In the United States women and gays made huge gains, and the various identity-based movements—feminist, gay, and race based—emerged vigorous, but the general student movement was finished. Although the Vietnam War finally ground to an end, and Richard Nixon was forced to resign the presidency, the 1970s were largely a time of defeat when the right accumulated power. Labour and the Democrats were on their way into twilight. For radicals the spirit of an insurgent class fused from its various fragments was no longer available. Instead, they were left with nostalgia for eras of struggle that they increasingly knew only at second or third hand.

The decay of the left's purchase on majoritarian politics helped rivet academic attention to popular culture. If one thought about youth culture properly, perhaps some sort of Marxist vision of history might be preserved! Perhaps youth culture would invigorate, cement, even ennoble the rising class bloc that would ultimately displace and overcome the ruling groups! At least popular culture was filled with oppositional spirit! If political power was foreclosed for the time being, the battlements of culture still remained to be taken! Or perhaps—if one really believed that the personal was the political—they had already been taken! Whatever the case, victories in popular culture might take the sting out of political defeat.

At the end of a decade of youthful rebellion, it was easiest to look to youth subcultures in the industrial countries for the emergence of disaffections that might amalgamate into an effective opposition to capitalism and racism. Culture, in this view, was a field of combat. The spirit of the moment was to define the combat in terms imported from political struggles. Cultural struggle was class struggle by other means. The grid of meaning that was discerned within (or imposed upon) popular culture was imported from radical politics. It had a teleology. It was not simply conflict but "contestation," a self-conscious means by which a quasi-class was becoming a quasi-class-for-itself. In fact, it was not simply contestation but *the* stark and classic contestation between forces of liberation and forces of repression. In the 1970s the early work of the Birmingham Centre for Contemporary Cultural Studies, especially its study of the "mugging" panic, concentrated on this coupled relationship: the meanings of rebellious youth activity experienced by the rebels themselves, alongside the repressive definitions imposed upon these activities by dominating media. If the bourgeois culture of the suites was hegemonic, and therefore oppressive, then the angrily antibourgeois culture of the streets was counterhegemonic, therefore resistant, and the class struggle was alive. Paul Willis's early work was saturated with ironic awareness that stances of dissidence among working-class boys might serve to integrate them all the more closely into lives of on-the-job subordination.[6] But the still-greater influence radiated from another Birmingham product, Dick Hebdige, who took a tendency already latent in earlier Birmingham work and codified it into a virtual equating of style with politics.[7] Hebdige's enthusiasm for dissonant symbolism refused to dampen radical hopes in corrosive baths of irony. In Hebdige style was insurgency because it was bricolage, and because bricolage pried symbols away from their original contexts, it was self-defining activity—"resistance."

From the late 1960s onward, as I have said, the insurgent energy was to be found in movements that aimed to politicize specific identities—racial minorities, women, gays. More generally, cultural studies set itself to discern "agency" among either marginalized or "ordinary" people—initiative and creativity on the part of people whom, it was said, academicians of conventional stripes overlooked or underestimated. If the "collective behavior" school of once-conventional sociology had classified insurgent movements as the functional equivalents of fads and fashions,[8] cultural studies now set out to peel movements away from fads, to take seriously what movement participants thought they were doing, and thereby to restore the dignity of the movements—only to end up, in the 1980s, reaggregating movements with fads by finding equivalent dignity in both spheres, so that, for example, dressing like Madonna or watching a talk show on family violence was upgraded to an act of "resistance" equivalent to demonstrating in behalf of the right to abortion. In this way cultural studies deepened the New Left symbiosis with popular culture. Eventually, the popular culture of marginal groups (punk, reggae, disco, feminist poetry, hip-hop) was promoted to a sort of counterstructure of feeling and even, at the edges, a surrogate politics—a sphere of thought and sensibility hypothetically insulated from the pressures of hegemonic discourse, of instrumental reason, economic rationality, class, gender, racial, and sexual subordination.

Cultural studies claimed that culture continued radical politics by other means. The idea was that cultural innovation was daily insinuating itself into the activity of ordinary people. Perhaps these millions had not actually been absorbed into the hegemonic sponge of mainstream popular culture! Perhaps they were objectively dissident after all—even sitting at home on their sofas. If "the revolution" had receded to the point of futility, it was depressing to contemplate (in the manner of the Frankfurt school) the victory of the culture imposed by overbearing media. ("The closing of the universe of discourse" was what Herbert Marcuse had said we were up against in his influential *One-Dimensional Man*—hardly an invitation to activism, whatever Marcuse's personal enthusiasms. Marcuse's closed universe was like Foucault's ubiquitous power—an all-embracing fate that willy-nilly reduced resistance to a hobby.) How much more reassuring to detect "resistance" saturating the pores of everyday life, as if the struggle against fascism flickered even in the inner pulp of the couch potato. The spread of the jargon-term *agency*, an arcane synonym for will and potency, underscores the preciousness of the quest. Eager to believe that the populace retained a potential for the right—that is, left—political engagement, left-wing academics resorted to a word that to most people smacked of something else: advertising or employment or travel.

In this spirit there emerged a welter of studies purporting to discover not only the "active" participation of audiences in shaping the meaning of popular culture but the "resistance" of those audiences to hegemonic frames of interpretation in a variety of forms—news broadcasts, romance fiction, television fiction, television in general, and many others.[9] Feminists were fascinated by the fictions and talk shows of daytime "women's television," seeing them as furthering a "discourse" of women's problems that men derogated as "merely" personal. The conventional dismissal of these shows as banal soap opera was said to follow from the patriarchal premise that what takes place within the four walls of the home is of less public significance than what takes place in a public sphere not so coincidentally established for the convenience of men. Observing the scale of the audiences for Oprah Winfrey and other public confessors, many in cultural studies upended the phenomenon by turning the definitions around. The largely female audiences for these shows would no longer be dismissed as distracted voyeurs but praised as active participants in the politicizing of crimes like incest and spousal abuse. It was less inspiring to think of them as confirming their normality with a brief vicarious acquaintanceship with deviance than to think of them as an avant-garde social movement.

In a word, cultural studies veered into populism.[10] Having been found worthy of attention by its practitioners, popular culture became worthy of attention by its students. Against the unabashed elitism of conventional literary and art studies, cultural studies affirmed an unabashed populism that derived intellectually from a sociological tendency in which all social activities matter, all are comprehensible, and all contain clues to the social nature of human beings. But this tendency in cultural studies goes further than noting the flows of popular culture and interpreting them. It seeks a political potential—a progressive one at that.[11] The object of attention is certified as worthy of attention not by being "the best that has been thought and said in the world" but by having been thought and said by and for "the people"—by a vast population or a subculture that is often, though not always, the cultural student's own group or one with which she or he identifies.

So the popularity of popular culture is what gives it value— and not only as an object of study. The sociological judgment that popular culture looms large in the lives of people blurs into a critical judgment that popular culture could not be popular were it not also valuable. Analysis slips into advocacy. Cultural studies wishes to overthrow hierarchy, but it is closer to the truth to say that what it actually does with hierarchy is invert it. What now certifies worthiness is the popularity of the object among people who are on the right side. Since they are good, what they like is good. In this intellectual milieu defenders of quality go on the defensive. The very words *literature* and *art* stick in the throats of cultural studies advocates, who can rightly point to shifting definitions of high and low art in the work of literary historians like Ian Watt, to say nothing of Michel Foucault on the genealogy of discursive frames or Raymond Williams on etymology.[12] But of course, in its imperviousness to questions of quality, cultural studies has ample company.

Cultural studies lacks irony. It wants to stand foursquare for the people against capitalism yet echoes the logic of capitalism.

The consumer sovereignty touted by a capitalist society as the grandest possible means for judging merit finds its reverberation among its ostensible adversaries—except that where the market flatters the individual, cultural studies flatters the group. What the group wants and buys is, ipso facto, the voice of the people. Popular creativity is alive, and the people are already in the process of liberation! Where once Marxists looked to factory organization as the prefiguration of "a new society in the shell of the old," today their heirs tend to look to sovereign culture consumers. David Morley, one of the key researchers in cultural studies and one of the most reflective, has himself recognized and deplored this tendency in audience studies.[13] He maintains that to understand that "the commercial world succeeds in producing objects . . . which do connect with the lived desires of popular audiences" is "by no means necessarily to fall into the trap . . . of an uncritical celebration of popular culture."[14] But where does one draw the line against the celebratory tendency when one is reluctant to criticize the cultural dispositions of the groups whom one approves? No wonder there is an arbitrariness to the assessments embedded in much published work in cultural studies—as if the researcher were straining to make the results conform to political needs. But academic studies charged with boosting morale may not serve the cause of enlightenment.

The populism of cultural studies prides itself on discharging a debt to politics. In the prevailing schools of cultural studies, to study culture is not so much to try to grasp cultural processes but to choose sides or, more subtly, to determine whether a particular cultural process belongs on the side of society's ideological angels. An aura of hope surrounds the enterprise, the hope (even against hope) of an affirmative answer to the question: Will culture ride to the rescue of liberation? There is defiance, too, as much as hope. Cultural studies means to cultivate insubordination. In this view marginalized groups defy hegemonic culture. If most of the academy remains hidebound, cultural studies will pry open its portals. By taking defiant popular culture seriously, one takes the defiers seriously and furthers their defiance. Cultural studies takes inventory, assessing the hegemonic import of culture and pinpointing potentials for "resistance." Is this mu-

sical style or that literary form "feminist" or "authentically La-
tino"? The field of possibilities is frequently reduced to two: for
or against the hegemonic. Or perhaps the prize goes to "hybridity"—as if subcultural combinations were automatically superior.
But the nature of hegemony, in its turn, is commonly defined
tautologically: that culture is hegemonic that is conducive to, or
promoted by, "the ruling group" or "the hegemonic bloc" and,
by the same token, that culture is "resistant" that is affirmed by
groups assumed (because of objective class position, gender, race,
sexuality, ethnicity, etc.) to be "marginalized" or "resistant." The
process of labeling is circular, since it has been predetermined
whether a particular group is, in fact, hegemonic or resistant.

The populism of cultural studies is fundamental to its allure.
To say that popular culture is worth scholarly attention is to say
that the people who render it popular are not misguided when
they do so: not fooled, not dominated, not distracted, not pas-
sive. If anything, the reverse: the premise is that popular culture
is popular because and only because the people find in it channels of desire, pleasure, empowerment. The people in their wisdom have erected a *worthy* partition, separating culture (good)
from conventional politics (bad), and then, magically, culture has
turned out to be politics—real politics, unofficial politics, deep
politics—after all. This premise is what gives cultural studies its
aura of political engagement—or, if nothing else, political consolation. To unearth reason and value, brilliance and energy in
popular culture is to affirm that the people, however embattled,
however divided, however battered, however fearful, however un-
employed, however drugged, have not been defeated. The cultural student, singing their songs, analyzing their lyrics, at the
same time sings their praises. However unfavorable the balance
of political forces, people succeed in living lives of vigorous resistance. Are communities of African Americans suffering? Well,
they have hip-hop—leave aside the question of whether all of
them want hip-hop in equal measure or what values it mobilizes
besides aggression and self-assertion.

The thirst for consolation explains the rise of academic cultural studies during precisely the years when the right held more
political power for a longer stretch than at any other time in gen-

erations. Consolation and embattlement led to the wishful notion that cultural studies, for all its frailty, amounted to a force combating right-wing power. To believe this one had to vulgarize the feminist notion that "the personal is political." In effect, one had to believe that "the cultural is political." In popular culture the opposition could find footing and breathing space, rally the powerless, defy the grip of the dominant ideas, isolate the powers that be, and prepare for a "war of position" against its dwindling ramparts. To dwell on the centrality of popular culture was good for morale. It certified the people and their projects. The assumption was that what held the ruling groups in power was their capacity to muffle, deform, paralyze, or destroy contrary tendencies. If a significant opposition were to exist, it first had to find a base in popular culture—and first also turned out to be second, third, and home plate as well, since popular culture was so much more accessible, porous, and changeable than the economic and political order.

With time, what began as compensation hardened into a tradition. Younger scholars gravitated to cultural studies because it was to them incontestable that culture *was* politics. To do cultural studies, especially in connection with identity politics, was the only politics they knew or respected. The contrast with the rest of the West is illuminating. In varying degrees left-wing intellectuals in France, Italy, Scandinavia, Germany, Spain, and elsewhere retain energizing attachments to Social Democratic, Green, and other left-wing parties. There, the association of culture with excellence and traditional elites remains strong. But in the Anglo-American world these conditions scarcely obtain. Here, in a discouraging time, popular culture emerges as a consolation prize. Throughout the English-speaking world of Europe, North America, and Australia, class inequality may have soared, ruthless individualism may have intensified, racial misery may have mounted, unions and social democratic parties may have reached an impasse, the organized left may have fragmented and its ideas blurred, but never mind. Attend to popular culture, study it with sympathy for the rewards that minorities find there, and one need not be unduly vexed by electoral defeat. One need not be rigorous about what one opposes and what one proposes in its place. Is capitalism the trouble? Is it the particular form of capitalism practiced by multinational corporations in a deregulatory era? Is it patriarchy (and is that the proper term for a society that has seen many improvements in the status of women)? Racism? Practitioners of cultural studies permit themselves their evasions. Speaking cavalierly of "opposition" and "resistance" permits—rather, cultivates—a certain sloppiness of thinking. You can identify with the left without having to face hard questions of political self-definition.

So the situation of cultural studies conforms to the contours of the past political generation. For economic and political ideas it substitutes a cheerleading approach to popular culture, with its cascading choices and technological marvels. Its cultivation of sensibility ratifies the wisdom of the prevailing withdrawal from practical politics. Seeking political energies in audiences who function qua audiences, rather than in citizens who function qua citizens, cultural studies stamps its seal of approval upon what is already a powerful tendency within industrial societies: popular culture as a surrogate for politics.

Indeed, cultural studies worships at the shrine of the marketplace. Its idea of the intellect's democratic commitment is to flatter the audience. Disdaining elitism, cultural studies helps erode the legitimacy of an intellectual life that cultivates assessments of value independent of popular taste. Trashing the canon, it deprives students of the chance—for once in their lives—to encounter culture that lives by values apart from the market. Whatever its radical gloss, cultural studies integrates itself nicely into a society that converts the need for distraction into one of its central industries and labels as "critics" those arbiters of taste whose business is to issue shopping advice to restless consumers.

Is there a chance of a modest redemption? Perhaps, if we imagine harder-headed, less wishful studies of culture that do not claim to be politics. A chastened realistic cultural studies would divest itself of pretensions. It would be less wishful about the world—and also about itself. Rigorous practitioners of cultural studies would rethink their premises. They would learn more about politics and history. They would deepen their knowledge of culture beyond the contemporary. When they study the contemporary, they would investigate cultural strands of which they do not necessarily approve. In the process they would appreciate better what culture, and cultural studies, do *not* accomplish. If we wish to do politics, let us organize groups, coalitions, demonstrations, lobbies, whatever: let us do politics. Let us not think that our academic pursuits are already that.

Notes

1. Present when Aronowitz made this announcement—at a conference organized by the history of consciousness program at the University of California, Santa Cruz—was Adam Michnik, a major intellectual figure in the Polish movement against communism, who naturally held a rather different idea of social movement and found the proceedings something between incomprehensible and laughable. His astonishment at what passed for political debate among American academics was more than idiosyncratic. It reflected an Eastern European's understanding of where the fundamental dividing line falls in politics: between civil society and the state.

2. Riesman, *The Lonely Crowd* (New Haven, Conn.: Yale University Press, 1950).

3. Gitlin, *Media Unlimited: How the Torrent of Images and Sounds Overwhelms Our Lives* (New York: Metropolitan/Holt, 2002).

4. Thompson, *The Making of the English Working Class* (New York: Pantheon, 1963).

5. On youth see Stuart Hall and Tony Jefferson, eds., *Resistance Through Rituals: Youth Subcultures in Post-War Britain* (London: Hutchinson, 1976); on television personalities see especially Stuart Hall, Ian Connell, and Lidia Curti, "The 'Unity' of Public Affairs Television," in *Working Papers in Cultural Studies*, vol. 9 (Birmingham, U.K.: Centre for Contemporary Cultural Studies, University of Birmingham, 1976), pp. 51–93; on television viewers see Dave Morley, *The "Nationwide" Audience* (London: British Film Institute, 1980).

6. Paul Willis, *Learning to Labour* (Farnborough, Hants, U.K.: Saxon House, 1977), and Willis, *Profane Culture* (London: Routledge and Kegan Paul, 1978).

7. Hebdige, *Subculture: The Meaning of Style* (London: Routledge, 1988).

8. Neil Smelser, *Theory of Collective Behavior* (London: Routledge and Kegan Paul, 1962).

9. On news see Morley, *The "'Nationwide" Audience;* on romance fiction see Janice Radway, *Reading the Romance* (Chapel Hill: University of North Carolina Press, 1984); on television fiction see Tamar Liebes and Elihu Katz, *The Export of Meaning* (New York: Oxford University Press, 1990), and Andrea Press, *Women Watching Television* (Philadelphia: University of Pennsylvania Press, 1991); and on television in general see John Fiske, *Television Culture* (London: Routledge, 1989).

10. See Jim McGuigan, *Cultural Populism* (London: Routledge. 1992).

11. The following revelation recorded by a leading British film theorist speaks volumes: "My own road to Damascus came over a decade ago when an entire fifteen-strong graduate class subscribed to the opinion that they would not outlaw clitoridectomy in other societies on the grounds that this would be the imposition of western norms." Colin MacCabe, "Mumbo-Jumbo's Survival instinct," www.opendemocracy.net/debates/article-1-66-2324.jsp (February 1, 2005).

12. Watt, *The Rise of the Novel: Studies in Defoe, Richardson, and Fielding* (Berkeley: University of California Press, 1957); Foucault, *The Order of Things: An Archaeology of the Human Sciences* (London: Tavistock, 1970); Williams, *Keywords: A Vocabulary of Culture and Society* (New York: Oxford University Press, 1976).

13. Morley, *Television, Audiences and Cultural Studies* (London: Routledge, 1992), pp. 10–41.

14. Ibid., p. 35.

6

The Values of Media, the Values of Citizenship, and the Values of Higher Education

What Media Cultivate

Talk about values is in the American grain, and so it has gone since 1776, when the United States was deliberately imagined as a nation distinguished by its ideals rather than by the nationality of its inhabitants. In principle, Americanness is a matter of principle. There is, of course, a recurrent nativist streak, which looks to ethnic or racial origin as a stand-in for qualification, but nevertheless, no other nation speaks so incessantly about values as the foundation of its existence.

Might it be that the rhetoric of values, repeated with a recurrent pounding of rostrums, conceals as much as it reveals? Realism requires that to know seriously the values of a society or a civilization, we should look beyond what people profess about what they value. To grasp the values of a society, or a civilization, we should look beyond what people say about what they believe, to what they do—and not only what they do when they are gathered up at ritual moments but, day after day, how they spend their time. The truth of a civilization is less what it professes than how it busies itself.

To an extraordinary degree the way this civilization spends its time is as spectators, listeners, recipients, and donors of communication. We spend our time in the presence of media.[1]

The nonstop arrival and flow of story and sound and image is a huge unacknowledged fact of our collective life. We prefer to think of ourselves as an information society, but this label simplifies the experience that takes place as the stories, songs, and images never cease to arrive. Sometimes we pay more attention and sometimes less, but all in all, we live among media to such a degree that time with media is the bulk of the time that people have at their disposal when they're not asleep or at work—and in fact they spend much of their time at work or on their way to or from work with media, underscoring the point.

In the course of about twenty-five years of writing about media, among other things, it often felt to me that the deepest truth about media was slipping through my fingers, something for which I didn't have an analytical category. While working on other projects, I sometimes collected note cards under the gaudy rubric "ontology," notes to myself about people's immersion in media. The note cards gathered dust.

What crystallized the conclusion that I defend here was a parable about a customs official. He goes to work on the border, and just after he arrives on the job he observes a truck rolling up to his customs booth. He asks the driver some questions, the man answers them, and the guard waves him through. The next day, somewhat to his surprise, the same truck driver pulls up, and this time the guard asks him the same questions, and the driver gives acceptable answers, and he waves him through. The next day the same driver is back. The guard's suspicion is growing. He tells the driver to get out of the cab. He pats him down. He can't find any contraband and waves him through. The next day the driver is back. This time the guard brings out some equipment. The day after that he brings in a colleague to help him search. This goes on for days, it goes on for weeks, it goes on for months, it goes on for years. Eventually, the guard is using the most sophisticated X-ray machines, sonar, technical measures hitherto unimagined. Never can he find any contraband. Finally, the guard reaches retirement age. Fast-forward to his last day on the job. Up rolls the truck driver. The official says, "Look, all these years I know you've been smuggling something. For my own satisfaction, please tell me what it is. I can never do you any harm now. I won't say a word. Just tell me, what have you been smuggling?" To which the answer is, of course, trucks.

The media have been in the habit of smuggling the habit of living with media.

In the media-saturated way of life, people derive multiple satisfactions from various kinds of experience that they have with media. Surely, one reason why people are reliant on media is that powerful and wealthy organizations accrue benefits through the process of marketing it. The attention of customers is the commodity that they sell to advertisers. One reason why people find the media omnipresent is that a grand effort is made to make them omnipresent. Many are the rewards that accrue to the attention-getting industries that deliver the most attractive goods. The effort of the attention getters amounts to the supply side of the story of media saturation.

But the supply side doesn't suffice for a comprehensive understanding of what media immersion accomplishes for us, as individuals, as a culture, and even as a civilization. While people are surely coaxed, and their preferences molded, in part, by their cultural environment, I cannot accept the notion that people are force-fed with what, after all, gives them pleasure. Americans are by no means exceptional in their reliance on popular culture. It's of some interest that in 1992, when Euro Disneyland opened outside Paris, and French intellectuals were signing petitions denouncing it as (in the words of one famous director) "a cultural Chernobyl," *Terminator II* sold five million tickets in France, a nation of fifty million. This didn't happen because Arnold Schwarzenegger stood outside the theater with an AK-47 herding everyone inside. Something is in it for the customers in media saturation: call it the demand side.

Consonant with our flattering image of ourselves is that we claim that we go to media in pursuit of information. The technically proficient like to herald themselves as the advance guard of the information society. But what is more important in driving people into the arms of media is that we look to have certain emotions and sensations. We're looking to feel. It seems so self-evident that only decades of scholarship could have missed it. I don't want to say that media experience is uniform, that reading the *Wall Street Journal* is the same as watching *Sesame Street*, or reading *Time* magazine, or viewing *The Simpsons*, or the latest reality show, or the CNN version of the war in Iraq, or listening to a top-ten single on the radio, or sending an instant message, or playing a video game. There are varieties of emotion and sensation attached to all these experiences. But what they have in common, it seems to me, is that they generate emotion or sensation of a type for which we hunger in the modern world: disposable emotion, emotion lite. Deep emotion would incapacitate you for feeling the next frisson. When you're deeply in love, or deeply in grief, you don't resort to a remote control device of the emotions in search of the next stimulus. You have the feeling, or you are the feeling, and the feeling has you. The kinds of feelings and sensations that we have from television, popular music, video games, the Internet, from most of the media that are common to us, these feelings are transitory and they are in a sense each a preparation for the next. If we were deeply satisfied, we wouldn't need the next. But we do need the next—or we feel we do.

Let me just throw out a few numbers to suggest the dimensions of the sort of relationship that I'm talking about. The figures that follow are for the United States, but Americans are not that far ahead of the rest of the developed world in our attachments to media. The average American television set is on for more than seven hours a day. The average individual is in the presence of a television set for about four and a half hours a day. We have a good study of the media habits of children aged two to eighteen, thanks to a solid survey underwritten by the Kaiser Family Fund in 1999. If we look at children aged two to eighteen, we will see that they spend, during an average day, six and three-quarter hours in contact with media, not counting homework. Of those six and three-quarter hours, they spend three-quarters of an hour reading (not counting homework). They spend the remaining six with television, recorded music, video games, and so on. More than two-thirds of American children have in their bedrooms a television set, a tape player, and a radio. Whether you live in a poor or a rich neighborhood, those figures for bedroom goods hold fairly constant. Black kids tend to watch more television, and boys are more likely than girls to have the equipment in their bedrooms, but the differences are less striking than the similarities. And all this is to speak strictly of in-house media: not the mall screens, billboards, Walkman and iPod modules, car radios, elevator music, and assorted other displays that accompany them as they move around their world.

Periodically, far-sighted observers anticipated that a society of this sort was coming. In the seventeenth century, for example, Pascal worried that kings would distract themselves from the proper pursuit of God with women, wine, and gambling. By today's lights virtually everyone in the rich societies can live like Pascal's distracted kings. The hunger for a way of spending time that makes limited demands and relieves a person from the burdens of normal existence—specifically, from the utilitarian calculation of everyday life—has become normal.

So much so that to challenge it is considered freakish. A while ago I was struck by the appearance on the front page of the *New York Times* of an article reporting that a man had been charged with credit card fraud in New Jersey and sentenced to ten months under house arrest without a television set. (At the time he owned seven.) What was this doing on the front page of the *New York Times?* His lawyers had gone to federal court, arguing that such a punishment constituted "cruel and unusual punishment." The editors of the *New York Times* thought this claim not only original but revelatory.[2]

Indeed. The media add up to a machinery of distraction, sensation, and stimulus, and yet institutionally the protections that the media enjoy, their legal and political position in our society, are predicated on a very different model of the purposes and significance of media—namely, one in which the media are carriers of debate for the self-government of a democratic citizenry. The First Amendment, which sanctions the freedoms that have become routine in the domain of the media, is predicated on an eighteenth-century model of political debate in which the media are intended not for steady and unbroken stimulus but for enlightenment. They are for the clarification of the public good.

This is surely one of the purposes of higher education: not only to train a skilled elite but to bolster the ability of the populace at large to conduct its collective affairs. Yet all educational institutions from the lowest to the highest discover that the official curriculum approved and passed down by school authorities, inscribed in textbooks, tested, graded, and succeeded by other curricula, contends with an informal and largely unacknowledged curriculum, the one that the students bring with them to school—a huge and interwoven set of songs, stories, gestures, terms, tones, slogans, icons, cartoon and celebrity names, figures, and gossip that they have derived from a virtually lifelong immersion in television, recorded music, radio, billboards, video games, and the other media that penetrate their everyday lives.[3] I am not saying that this unacknowledged curriculum is all that our students experience or know. A great deal of thought and imagination is bound up in their lives elsewhere—in the play that they undertake beyond media, their sports, reading, informal home lessons, family contact, religious activity, and so on. But to a large and growing degree their sense of the world is bound up with media and the emotions and sensations that they find in their contacts with media. They draw much of their shared vocabulary from media. The heroes that bind them are likely to be media celebrities, drawn mainly from the worlds of entertainment and sports.

It is beyond dispute that the informal curriculum of popular culture absorbs much of our students' mental attention. They bring televisions as well as computers and elaborate musical equipment to their dorm rooms. They carry digital phones, with instant messaging and (increasingly) camera adjuncts. They are everywhere in the presence of advertising. This ensemble contributes mightily to the web of social associations that binds them to one another. A welter of items, associations, and fascinations circulates through all the media of our time and then through peer groups, making jingles, themes, names, styles, logos, and so on familiar to them—and not only familiar but *interesting*.

The sum of nonstop image machinery, the whole nonstop sound track—these have been with the young from their earliest ages. As a result boredom is anathema, whence the media of preference must be speedy and sensational, full of surprises and rapid shifts. Trivia are tailored for weightlessness. "Dead air" is deadly. Movement is all. Sense gratification must be within reach, always. In the visual media edits come quickly—in music videos and commercials, frequently several per second. Sports are sped up by simultaneous stats, animations, and instant replays streaming across and punctuating the screen, so that even such a viscous spectacle as baseball becomes an explosion of dazzling segments. While human bodies run up against limits in their capacity to race, bend, and otherwise delight, animation does not. Music will be percussive, dominated by rhythmic pulsation. Electronic rumbles and drums drive emotional effects, bass notes producing an aura of menace, strings a whiff of cheer. Stories are conflictful, images kinetic. Many media tales have morals and may kindle a certain order of moral reflection, but usually the morals of the tale emerge quickly and demand rapid resolution.

Much of what streams through the media is funny—often self-consciously so. Jokes come thick and fast, or are supposed to, pitched at the average level of early teens. Physical humor, pratfalls, and goofiness are plenteous. Popular culture serves as the repertory on which popular culture itself draws, so that there is little or no recognition that any more demanding, worthier culture might exist. In the last generation a recognition of the omnipresence of popular culture, as well as its foolishness, is built into popular culture in the form of sarcasm and tongue-in-cheek attitudes. Cartoons that mock the rest of popular culture (most brilliantly in *The Simpsons,* the exception that proves the rule), ads that smirk at other ads, soap opera characters who selectively disparage popular culture, magazines and websites that mercilessly unmask others—these are the common currency. Stupidity is subject to mockery, too, but in a way that suggests that what is wrong with stupidity is that it isn't hip and that those who rise above stupidity are, more than likely, snobs.

This is the condition of the bulk of popular culture and remains so even if the observer does not sink into a chiding voice. There are of course exceptions where intelligence is not mocked. The best to be said for this culture is that it brings a certain diversity into parochial households, cultivates curiosity, and recommends tolerance. But to expect that expectations of popular culture are tidily put away the moment the student walks into the classroom or opens a textbook is naive—insupportably so.

Casual violence, however misunderstood, is a common value in popular culture. On this score video games considerably compound the effects of network television, and video games are compounded by videocassettes, heavy metal, and rap music. The deeper significance of all the casual violence is not self-evident; of causal links to violence in the real world there is little serious evidence and much counterevidence. My own view is that the importance of media violence lies largely in the sensory experience that it generates, not in the dire behavioral effects popularly attributed to it. The evidence from laboratory studies, limited as it is as a predictor of effects in the outside world, suggests that violent images cultivate both anger and indifference, neither of which is conducive to the intellectual receptivity, disciplined competence, and methodical deliberation that study—or, for that matter, citizenship—requires.

In other words, violence in the media is best addressed as a commonplace feature of the lives that young people actually live, not a trigger for violence in the actual world beyond media. The replicas of violence constitute themselves a sort of real experience, a part of the life that young people live, a part that registers as cognitive and emotional. It is not an intimation of violence to be performed at some other time or place, it is *already here* in one's daily world. While violence in the media pours forth without a corresponding uptick in the violence of the actual world, it does make the world—*at least the world of human connection with the media themselves,* a world that young people live in during many hours a day—appear casually cruel. In these everyday adventures aggressiveness is the common currency of life. One had better get used to it.

Violence is only one of the regular crudities. Everyday media are soaked in coarseness of many sorts. Primitive jeers, double entendres, easy jokes about body functions feature regularly in many programs radiated to young people through network sitcoms, MTV, the Comedy Channel, and other commercial sources, as well as video games (which now outgross movies, in both senses of *outgross*) and Internet entertainments. The sexual innuendo of music videos is hard to miss, whence its huge adolescent appeal. Overall, though, probably more prevalent than sexual suggestiveness is the crude style evident in vocabulary, look, gestures—the whole expressive repertory of popular culture. The full range of human emotions is collapsed into the rudimentary alternatives of "love" and "hate," "cool" and "gross." The media take the side of the simple over the complex, the id over the superego, the pleasure principle over the reality principle, the popular over the unpopular.

All in all, then, the media promote emotional payoffs—and expectations of payoffs. The rewards are immediate: fun and excitement. Images and sounds register in the here and now. They are supposed to feel good—this is the expectation. They make a cardinal promise: you have a right not to be bored. Yet the media must not feel *too* good for *too* long, because part of their goodness is that they change, yield to the next, and we know it. Accordingly, our students have become accustomed to feel feelings with a particular quality: feelings that are relatively disposable, fast-rising and fast-fading, excitements and expectations that readily yield (and are expected to yield) to other fast-rising and fast-fading feelings, excitements, and expectations. Young people expect their images and sound tracks not only to cause enjoyment but to change. They expect jolts of sensation, surges of unexpected (yet, paradoxically, predictably unexpected) feelings. They expect to change the channel—or fast-forward the tape, or search out a different song on the CD or the iPod—if it does not please them.

Thus the unacknowledged curriculum readies them not only for sensation but for interruption. Interruption is a premise of contemporary perception. It is no small part of the experience of media. Interruption—and the expectation of it—is built into the media's own texture. Programs interrupt themselves. In commercials, trailers, and other filler, one story interrupts another—expedited by channel switching and the variety of distractions (talking, eating, chatting on the phone, exchanging "buddy messages" on line, and so on) that children build into their media experience.

Interruption is even built into content. In the spelling lessons of *Sesame Street*, as in the commercials after which it was patterned, in action movies as in video games, in music videos as in disk jockey chit-chat, in sportscasting as in news, the young expect split screens, moving logos, and quick cuts, even if some continuity may be supplied by the sound track. The acceleration of editing during the past generation is striking, with images jump-cutting to other images in a split second. The contrast with the past is plain whenever one sees a movie more than twenty years old—how static it looks! Finally, within the unedited frame is the now-normal glide or zoom or, in any case, movement of the image itself, the product of a handheld camera, or one on a dolly or Steadicam. In media the "story line" turns out to be jagged. The expectation of immediate but disposable rewards has become normal.

Interruption becomes routine. Interference leads to multitasking as the young become accustomed to dividing their attention. Media frequently come to them simultaneously or near-simultaneously—and they expect them to come that way. The habit of switching is partly a function of the convenience of switching. Thanks to the remote control device, one of the most underestimated of contemporary technologies, they may conveniently graze among two or three television channels in rapid alternation. They may switch between a video game and a soap opera or sports event, and so on.

For this reason, among others, I do not want to argue that when the young attend to the media of popular culture, they are necessarily deeply attentive. To the contrary: they tune out much of the time. They select what they attend to. They retain unevenly. Sometimes they focus and sometimes not. Those who approve of the habit of simultaneous media viewing and listening refer to the cognition that this practice demands as "parallel processing." Those who disapprove consider it distraction. But however one evaluates this common condition of half-attention, it is not the focus that is required for intellectual mastery—learning a language, performing a complex computation, grasping the contours of history, assessing rival explanations of a given phenomenon, assessing the moral implications of complex realities. It is not a mood conducive to education—or citizenship. Are we not too distracted, or even addled, for such concentration?

Education and the Values of Citizenship

Against this background—the texture of everyday life in a media-saturated society—the values of education for citizenship become indispensable, all the more so in an era when higher education is the almost automatic vehicle for advancement.

For students, as for others, popular culture has recreational uses. Escape from rigors and burdens is, after all, its point. But the sheer profusion of popular culture in the lives of the young has a larger implication: the informal curriculum of immediate gratification obstructs education for citizenship—just as it obstructs the analytical work of education across the board.

Education's prime obligation to the public weal in a democratic society is to improve the capacity of citizens to govern themselves. For now I leave in suspension the question of the degree to which the good citizen is a direct participant in the decisions that affect his or her life—the ideal enshrined as participatory democracy in the 1960s—or, on the other hand, one who (in Michael Schudson's term) "monitors" the decisions of public bodies and intervenes in public affairs only occasionally, in particular when they make decisions that offend ideals or interests.[4] I take it as axiomatic, in either event, that higher education has a distinct and significant part to play in forming and bolstering the capacity for citizenship. The growth of higher education makes colleges and universities steadily more promising—or disappointing, as the case may be—in their potential for public improvement. But colleges and universities can discharge this duty only when they combat the distraction induced by media saturation.

Some, mainly on the left, would argue that an obligation of higher education is to mobilize activists. Now, there is much to be said for the proposition that activism is the lifeblood of democracy. Toward that end, as part of their democratic mission, universities are obliged to mobilize students to register to vote and, subsequently, actually to vote. (The youth vote has declined precipitously since the mid-1970s, as has the percentage of students who read newspapers regularly.) Universities as institutions must shield the rights of dissenters, students, and faculty alike.[5]

But beyond such fundamental service to democracy, universities ought not to be entrusted with any political mobilization in particular. Institutions of learning are forums, not parties. If they were to endorse a position, which would it be, and who would decide? If public opinion shifted, or were heavily polarized, wouldn't the university need to adjust its position or risk being torn apart? Universities' primary mission would be in danger of succumbing to ephemera.

So universities ought to embrace citizenship, not particular uses of citizenship. They short-circuit the educational process and damage their commitment to reason if they officially advocate beyond a bare minimum, for advocacy cuts short the deliberative process that is their proper charge. Position taking would compel ideological minorities to concede that their participation in reflection and deliberation is fruitless because the issue has already been decided. Moreover, activists ought to realize that endorsements are useless on practical grounds. What reason is there to believe that universities can actually shift public opinion outside their walls?

Mainly, universities serve bedrock purposes of higher education in a democracy when they spur reasoned participation in politics and the accumulation of knowledge to suit. For the work of arousing and channeling passions there are political organizations, parties, and movements. Education has a more precise responsibility: to cultivate reason and to deepen understanding of the world. No other institution is dedicated to these functions. In fact, the political sphere is in many ways dedicated to undermining them, as, in their own ways, are media. Yet reason and understanding, the university's own specialized charge, are imperative. There is no time when this is not so. But a time like the present, with unreason on the march, especially needs an infusion of knowledge into the political domain. To judge foreign policy, energy programs, terrorist threats, ecological problems, questions of economics, and so forth requires not just committed but knowledgeable citizens. Truly, the United States has suffered in recent years from failures of intelligence in more than one sense. Universities, no less than other institutions, have cultivated complacency.

For citizenly as well as strictly educational purposes, then, higher education ought to cultivate a disciplined curiosity about the world and an enthusiasm for careful disputation. Toward these ends, schooling needs to counter the impulsive, hyperkinetic, associational, trivia-centered relation to images and sounds that the bulk of the media offer. Colleges and universities ought to be arenas for robust speech, where students are encouraged not only to reinforce views they already hold but—knowledgeably and logically—to challenge and modify them. An atmosphere conducive to reflection is a prerequisite for education in civic preparedness, as also for learning in its own right. Where else in modern life is such an atmosphere to be found, or created, responsive to social needs that are not the needs of the market? If not in colleges and universities, hardly anywhere.

Beyond training in specialized crafts, institutions of higher learning exist in significant part to deepen understanding of intellectual traditions—of science, the humanities, and social sciences alike. Toward this end, the spirit of higher learning benefits when students are, for some of their college careers, immersed in a common curriculum. The decisive reason is not that the standard lists of canonical texts deserve to be engraved in granite strictly by virtue of their longevity (a circular argument) or their Westernness (not an argument in behalf of their logic-inducing potential). It is that the student body's shared exposure to central literary and philosophical texts and methods of argument enlarges the community of reason. It widens the circle of shared conversation. It challenges parochialisms of all sorts—including the demographic and subcultural niches preferred by the market as well as the specializations preferred by the professions. Not only does a common curriculum help overcome the intellectual narrowness that accompanies specialization. The core experience also helps cultivate citizens who might be capable of rising above private and group interest to work toward a common good. A core curriculum aerates elites and tends, over time, to substitute meritocratic principle for inherited cultural capital.

So a common curriculum, including political philosophy (and thus defenses as well as criticisms of democratic theory), has citizenly as well as intellectual uses. These uses extend beyond the makeup of the curriculum's subjects to the cultivation of reason itself. In particular, the atmosphere of higher education should cultivate an awareness—controversial in today's climate—that an argument is different from an assertion or an opinion. An argument is obliged to confront its contraries: to engage them, not to ignore them. An argument ought to confront its contraries at their strong points, not their weak points. An argument is not the simple pressing of a point, as in the shoutfests that characterize radio, television, and movie punditry. We cannot speak of argument without evidence and logic. Yet for years, while teaching at Berkeley, New York University, and Columbia, I have noticed how frequently students have difficulty understanding what an argument is. Many, asked to make an argument on a particular subject, express an opinion—or even an emotion ("I feel that"). Many high school graduates arrive at the university without learning what an argument is. Plainly, the whole educational system is in default.

Citizenship requires more than reason, but the public sphere cannot dispense with reason without making a mockery of the democratic idea. Yet, just as the torrent of media washes away the careful sifting and winnowing that reason requires, the conduct of politics today is inimical to the reasoning arts. A reputation for excessive knowledge is "wonkish." A reputation for verbal stumbling establishes the common touch and certifies "likeability." The anti-intellectualism of American life, of which Richard Hofstadter wrote tellingly forty years ago, has not diminished even as the proportion of the adult population attending colleges and universities and acquiring degrees, even advanced degrees, has grown.[6]

In principle, Americans ought to be more thoughtful and knowledgeable than ever before. If years spent in school are the right measure, we have surely become better educated. Between 1960 and 2003 the percentage of the adult population that graduated from high school more than doubled, from 41 to 85 percent of those aged twenty-five and older. During the same period the percentage of college graduates in the adult population almost quadrupled, to 27.2 percent of those aged twenty-five or older.[7]

How knowledgeable are Americans, then? Comparative data on political knowledge are scarce, but to take one salient subdivision of knowledge, Americans' knowledge of foreign affairs ranks low in multinational assessments—sometimes startlingly so. In a 1994 Times Mirror survey in which the same five questions about international facts were asked of people in seven countries—the United States, Canada, France, Germany, Italy, Spain, and the United Kingdom—Americans ranked sixth, surpassing only the Spaniards. Thirty-seven percent of Americans could not answer any of the questions correctly, and only 15 percent could answer at least four of the five (as opposed to 58 percent in Germany and 34 percent in Italy).[8] American knowledge of world geography ranked near the bottom in a *National Geographic* survey of ten countries.[9]

A compendious survey by Michael X. Delli Carpini and Scott Keeter comes to this general conclusion: "In spite of significant increases in educational attainment, aggregate levels of political knowledge are about the same today as they were forty to fifty years ago, raising the possibility that the schools today are less effective at transmitting political information or stimulating political engagement."[10] Or at the least: whatever knowledge benefits schools succeed in imparting are outweighed by forces that undermine knowledge.

The public sphere is less a theater of debate than a theater of repetition, professionalized into the imperative of staying "on message." Politics has taken more than a leaf from the advertising manual of driving the point home by pounding in a Unique Selling Proposition[11]—it has taken the whole book. Talk radio and punditry excel in podium pounding, not argument. Much of our politics follows suit and not only in election campaigns: the Supreme Court's nonsensical decision in 2000's *Bush v. Gore* is a case in point. Presidential speech can skirt logic and evidence without evident penalty. Zbigniew Brzezinski, former national security adviser to Jimmy Carter, pointed out in April 2003 that in the eighteen months since September 11, 2001, President Bush spoke the words "either you're with us or with the terrorists" ninety-nine times. To state what ought to be obvious: the repetition of such remarks is not an argument. It is a declaration meant to stop an argument. Declamation by fiat presumes that an argument has already been made and won.

Declamation by fiat is Bush's presidential manner, though it is scarcely unique to him. On more than one occasion he could proudly declare, "I don't do nuance" without chastisement from most of his supporters, who seemed proud that his ostensibly from-the-gut straight-shooter performance brooked no complications. On June 17, 2004, Bush said: "The reason I keep insisting that there was a relationship between Iraq and Saddam and al Qaeda: because there was a relationship between Iraq and al Qaeda."[12] (He went on to cite the charge that Iraqi intelligence officers met with Osama bin Laden in Sudan in the 1990s, as if such contacts were ipso facto proof of collusion.) Bush's repeated yoking of September 11 terrorists and Saddam Hussein into the same sentence, without ever exactly making an argument about the nature of their connection, was a surrogate for logic. In this, as in many other of his pronouncements, Bush was resorting to the associative clamor of television commercials, as in: sexy woman fondling car = if you drive this car, she'll fondle you. A public official who asserts and reasserts in this manner without engaging contrary evidence is a bully, though many bullies are more glib than Bush. Perhaps because at some deep level he knows his weakness, Bush aims to win by overpowering dissent rather than engaging it. Whether such rhetorical performances reflect Bush's own thought process or his tactics for driving a point home, the result is not debate. It is propaganda.

To judge from published accounts Bush's intellectual process in private seems to match his propagandistic manner in public. According to former Treasury Secretary Paul O'Neill, as quoted in Ron Suskind's *The Price of Loyalty: George W. Bush, the White House, and the Education of Paul O'Neill*, the president did not read reports. Unlike Richard Nixon and Gerald Ford, under whom O'Neill had also served, Bush did not solicit rival opinions from his advisers. At meetings, O'Neill said, "the President is like a blind man in a roomful of deaf people. There is no discernible connection."[13] Christine Todd Whitman, formerly in charge of Bush's Environmental Protection Administration, "never heard the President analyze a complex issue, parse opposing positions, and settle on a judicious path. In fact, no one—inside or outside the government, here or across the globe—had heard him do that to any significant degree."[14] "With his level of experience," O'Neill told Suskind, "I would not be able to support his level of conviction."[15]

My point is not simply that a graduate of Yale University and Harvard Business School can conduct the public business in this manner—though slapdash governance is appalling enough. It is that in the United States at the turn of the twenty-first century the refusal, or inability, to reason is no disqualification for the presidency. In 2000 almost half the American electorate were willing to vote for an unreflective propagandist, although he had already demonstrated his illogic and evasiveness during the campaign. (In 2004 a bit more than half were willing to confirm his fitness for leadership, many of them on the strength of indefensible opinions on the facts of the Iraq war.[16]) Of course, if mainstream campaign journalists had not favored the story line that *Al Gore* was the prevaricator while George Bush was the amiable yahoo, they might have helped voters spot Bush's deceptions and evasions and so made it harder for him to sell his plain-folks brand.[17]

Disrespect for serious standards of political argument prevails throughout public life. In our debased state of political discourse, one of the most damning insults is the charge of two-sidedness: "flip-flopping," "waffling." What is being implicitly valued is consistency of opinion, which has come to stand for steadiness of nerve and reliability of character. In many situations steadiness is a virtue, indeed. But there is the further implication that changing one's mind is a mark of untrustworthiness.

Two things are wrong with this claim—two things that ought to be elementary. First, circumstances do not, as a rule, repeat. If it makes sense to fight a war under conditions A, B, and C, does it make sense to fight a war under conditions A, B, and D, or A, D, and E, or D, E, and F? As soon as the circumstances differ, the war differs, and therefore so does the justification for war. So to have favored the first war and not the second, or the second and not the first, may not be a sign of flip-flopping or inconsistency at all but of pragmatic ability to read situations as they deserve to be read: with care.

Then, too, during the course of public life in a democracy one encounters many contrary views. How is one to manage differences? Who is entitled to disregard views that are apparently delivered with logic and evidence? Only a tyrant is impervious to the dispositions of others. Any legislator must negotiate. So must most executives. In the process they discover in experience what they may already have half-realized in principle: that public positions often rest on different sets of evidence or different standards of evaluation. It makes sense to look at evidence that one might have disregarded. It makes sense to consider the values implicit in others' positions as well as one's own. The refusal to reconsider one's views is blindness—and to put it this way is to be uncharitable to blindness.

If one goal of public life is to improve the capacity of citizens and their representatives to govern their affairs, then whether one's side has won is but one measure of the success of a debate. The question is also whether the protagonists have learned anything in the process. What they learn in the current situation, both in substance and in method, can only help improve their capacity to address the next situation, for politics, like education and indeed the rest of life, is sequential. Education is of the essence. Learning from the defeated can take place under judicious rules in a properly run classroom, where those who hold unpopular views are encouraged to defend them, those who are uncertain are encouraged to understand better the grounds of their uncertainty, and students may experiment with unfamiliar or seemingly outré views.

Finally, higher education is obliged not only to cultivate habits of mind conducive to democratic debate but other habits as well—habits of emotion, sensibility, and (as principled conservatives would insist) character. In an era of high-speed media and trivial experience, what institution if not the university will acquaint students with the pleasures of argumentative care, the duties of open reflection, and the complex uses of what the critic Robert Hughes has called "slow art"?[18] On the subject of art much deserves to be said, but it ought to be self-evident that the greatest work is more likely to elicit depths of pity and terror than lightweight work. The complexity of motives and the torments of unintended consequences hold powerful lessons for public conduct. It is better to study *The Brothers Karamazov* than to study *General Hospital*. There is more to be derived from a production of *Hamlet* than a production of *Desperate Housewives*. Call it the intellectual sublime—and if that strikes you as an embarrassment, the embarrassment is a tribute to the power of the market. A curriculum that credits the sublime cannot be left to the vagaries of popular taste, for popular taste answers to other criteria, including the sheer inertia of the available. In composing a curriculum, the authority of teachers should not be surrendered to the commercial judgments that mold popular taste.

For again: the media's business is to stimulate emotion and sensation that generate instant payoffs measurable in the marketplace. Because their sole criterion of success is market preference, the prime question for them is always—*always*—whether they can get customers to pay attention. This commitment leaves the realm of emotion impoverished. I can get you to pay attention: I simply have to make a loud noise. But the sensibility of a self-governing society needs more from its collective emotional life than temptation or titillation. It needs patience. It needs to appreciate the sublime. It needs to savor (and sometimes solve) the complex. It needs to instruct in the overcoming of impulse. It needs to teach how to evaluate desire and know the difference between desirability and morality. It needs to teach how to make sense of duties when duties conflict. To glib answers it brings complication and further questions. To the shallowness of the moment it brings the subsoil of history. To the casualness of everyday talk it brings the discipline of seasoned judgment.

In sum, higher education has the burden of advancing the intellectual and moral side of citizenship. This obligation pits education against the noise of the media and against the pettiness, parochialism, and corruption of propaganda and politics. It deepens the educational mission. It enrolls higher education in the defense of the society's highest values. It is not a mission that can be offloaded onto any other institution. It is partisan only in the sense of a commitment to improve the common life. But this is a partisanship of which we have precious little today. If higher education abdicates its authority in order to float on popular tides, it defaults, and the common life weakens, whether the public knows it or not.

Notes

1. The following discussion recapitulates some passages from my *Media Unlimited: How the Torrent of Images and Sounds Overwhelms Our Lives* (New York: Metropolitan/Holt, 2002).

2. Benjamin Weiser, "A Sentence of No TV? Unusual, Yes, but Cruel?" *New York Times*, March 7, 2002, p. A1. In the event, a federal appeals court found in favor of the criminal in question (Benjamin Weiser, "House Arrest Doesn't Bar Watching TV, Court Rules," *New York Times*, October 24, 2002, p. B5.)

3. The following discussion of the unacknowledged curriculum draws on my essay "Teaching in the Torrent of Popular Culture," in Diane Ravitch and Joseph P. Viteritti, eds., *Kid Stuff: Marketing Sex and Violence to America's Children* (Baltimore: Johns Hopkins University Press, 2003), pp. 19–38.

4. Michael Schudson, *The Good Citizen: A History of American Civic Life* (New York: Basic Books, 1998), pp. 294–314, esp. p. 311.

5. For a strong defense of this mission by a former president of Kent State University, see Michael Schwartz, "The Place of Dissent in Inquiry, Learning, and Reflection," *Peace and Change* 21, no. 2 (April 1996): 169–81.

6. Richard Hofstadter, *Anti-Intellectualism in American Life* (New York: Alfred A. Knopf, 1963).

7. U.S. Census Bureau, *Statistical Abstract of the United States, 2003* (Washington, D.C. : U.S. Department of Commerce, 2004), no. 212.

8. Michael X. Delli Carpini and Scott Keeter, *What Americans Know About Politics and Why It Matters* (New Haven, Conn.: Yale University Press, 1997), p. 90, table 2.8. The questions were: "Who is the president of Russia?" "Which country is threatening to withdraw from the nonproliferation treaty?" "Who is Boutros Boutros Ghali?" "Which ethnic group has conquered much of Bosnia?" "With which group have the Israelis recently reached a peace accord?"

9. Cited in Henry Milner, *Civic Literacy: How Informed Citizens Make Democracy Work* (Lebanon, N.H.: University Press of New England, 2002), p. 58.

10. Delli Carpini and Keeter, *What Americans Know*, p. 199.

11. Rosser Reeves, *Reality in Advertising* (New York: Alfred A. Knopf, 1961).

12. Dana Milbank, "Bush Defends Assertions of Iraq–Al Qaeda Relationship," *Washington Post*, June 18, 2004, p. A9.

13. Ron Suskind, *The Price of Loyalty: George W. Bush, the White House, and the Education of Paul O'Neill* (New York: Simon and Schuster, 2004), pp. 148–49.

14. Ibid., p. 114.

15. Ibid., p. 325.

16. Steven Kull et al., "The Separate Realities of Bush and Kerry Supporters," October 21, 2004, Program on International Policy Attitudes at the University of Maryland, www.pipa.org/OnlineReports/Pres_Election_04/Report10_21_04.pdf (March 14, 2005).

17. To take one of a myriad examples, in the presidential debate of October 17, 2000, Bush said: "If I'm the president . . . people will be able to take their HMO insurance company to court. That's what I've done in Texas and that's the kind of leadership style I'll bring to Washington." In fact, as governor Bush vetoed the patients'-bill-of-rights measure passed by the Texas legislature in 1995. Passed again by a veto-proof majority, it become law without his signature in 1997. See Jake Tapper, "Spin Room: Spinning the Third Presidential Debate," CNN, October 18, 2000, and Charles Lane, "A 'Flip-Flop' on Patients' Right to Sue?" *Washington Post*, April 5, 2004, p. A15. At the time the *New York Times* corrected Bush's lie on p. A29 (Jim Yardley, "Taking Credit for Patients' Rights Where It's Not Necessarily Due," *New York Times*, October 18, 2000, p. A29). None of the three major television networks corrected Bush's lying braggadocio at all. As president Bush did nothing to pass a patients' bill of rights.

18. Robert Hughes, "A Bastion Against Cultural Obscenity," *Guardian*, June 3, 2004, www.guardian.co.uk/arts/features/story/0,11710,1230169,00.html (March 14, 2005).

III. The Intellectuals and the Flag

To tell the truth, September 11, 2001, jammed my mental circuits, and I spent much of the ensuing year trying to get them unjammed, first of all, and, second, trying to make sense of both the jolts and the jamming and to learn from them. This was as much an intellectual as an emotional undertaking. Resisting what is called "closure," I did not shy from bewilderment, from unprecedented feelings and thoughts, whole shelves stocked with cans of worms. I did not try to dispel my immediate feelings, horror and astonishment, because feelings can be links to reality, even if sometimes they throw you for a loop. Through my emotions I found myself in contact with—thinking about—questioning—and taken by—patriotism, and rethinking what intellectuals are good for and where they have let us down.

Proximity was not the cause. It wasn't that I and my family were in danger directly—we lived a mile north of the ruins of the Twin Towers, a sizable distance, as these things go, though close enough to see and hear the second explosion. A day and a night later, and for weeks to come, we were breathing the World Trade Center, the tons of acrid smoke, the vaporized remnants of thousands of computers, copy machines, phones, glass and steel, carpets and desks, asbestos, God knows what—corpses, too, though it took time to realize that. But the fumes of catastrophe don't make you rethink your principles. Fear—fear that this one-time event might not turn out to be a one-time event—fear comes closer to accomplishing that. But fear was only one feeling and there were others, surprising ones. Love, for example.

Thinking about that crystalline, desperate morning forever enshrined (and trivialized) by two numbers, I have tried to hold on to the astonishment and deepen it with reflection, not to flee from the shock. Experience that astonishes is not the sole truth but it is an indispensable truth—the truth of "wild history," in the historian Richard Slotkin's phrase, history that did not have to happen but that, once having happened, changes not only the future but the history that happened before.

My memories are of strangers and their losses but no less of solidarities. I think of a distraught young woman, red-haired, staggering up the sidewalk from the direction of the vanished Twin Towers, a continuous cascade of tears flowing down her face. I think of the handbills posted everywhere in lower Manhattan, the photos of the missing, *Have you seen* —? the desperate pleas to call this or that phone number, the candles burning on the sidewalks next to the fire stations, the hand-printed signs: Thank You to Our Heroic Fire Fighters. I recall a homeless woman on the subway declaring her sympathy for my wife, whose home, after all, was a mile from the rubble. Strangers wished each other good luck. It's not too much to say that I, and they, felt love for each other—love of a people who would endure. I think of mourners and mutual aid, in other words, not of the dead themselves. I also think of an open mike in Union Square where people started debating the U.S. response, people who disagreed vehemently but were willing to hear each other out.

I did not, as they say, "lose anyone." But I hope it does not sound either callous or self-congratulatory to say that in those awful days I *found* people—and a people to whom I belonged. The afternoon of September 14, my wife and I walked down to the perimeter of the ruins along the West Side of lower Manhattan and fell in with a crowd that was greeting and applauding rescue workers—police, fire fighters, phone and gas company people, ironworkers and welders, most driving slowly northward out of the smoking Ground Zero area as other trucks drove south, heading in. Some came trudging out of the zone, their boots caked in gray ash. Some people came around handing out pictures of loved, lost ones.

Out of the zone of ruins walked a man and woman in their early thirties, handsome, clear-eyed, wearing yellow slickers and boots. They were trying to figure out how to get to the subway. We advised on directions and fell in with them. Mary and Dean had driven down from Syracuse, 250 miles away, to volunteer and had just spent thirty-six hours in the belt of destruction, digging in rubble, dispersing whenever horns sounded to signal that buildings were in danger of collapse. They'd been directing themselves, more or less. Now the federal managers were coming in to take over.

They said it hadn't been easy to get into the damage zone: in fact, they'd had to trick their way in. They had reported to the main volunteer depot at the Javits Convention Center a mile and a half north. Mary, an image consultant at a cosmetic company, had some therapeutic experience and wanted to work with children. They found three hundred people lined up in front of them. So they attached themselves to an upstate fire company, got their yellow slickers, boots, and smoke-protection masks, and made their way to Ground Zero. They didn't know George W. Bush had made his appearance that afternoon (or that he'd been given a far less vigorous reception than Mayor Giuliani), nor were they impressed. At the time they'd been catching a couple of hours' sleep. Soaked by the first rain in days, they'd gone first to the shell of a nearby hotel, but there was a stench, and somebody walked up and told them not to sleep near the bodies.

I asked Dean what he thought the United States ought to do now. "We have to do something," he said, "but it's not easy. We have to be careful about retaliating. We need diplomatic pressure. We can't go bomb a lot of innocent people. *Then we've done what they've done.*" That same week I was also struck by a third-generation New Jersey flag shop owner, Gary Potervone, who was interviewed on ABC. He said that he sold twenty-seven thousand flags in a single day, adding: "It's not like the Gulf War. That was, 'Get 'em, get 'em.' This is more solidarity. I'm very happy to see true patriotism. This is so much warmth."

I loved these strangers, and others I met in those days, and didn't feel mawkish about it—these new, less aggressive New Yorkers, speaking in hushed voices, or so it seemed, lining up to give blood at the local hospitals, disappointed that no one was collecting any; the cabbies driving in unaccustomed silence, all the gratuitous horns shut down for a change; New Yorkers without their carapaces. I took inspiration from the patriotic activists who seem to have brought down Flight 93 over Pennsylvania and saved the White House or the Capitol. They hadn't waited for authorities to define their patriotism for them. They were not satisfied with symbolic displays. It dawned on me that patriotism was the sum of such acts.

The night of September 11, in search of clarity and shoring up, I reread George Orwell's 1945 essay, "Notes on Nationalism," wherein Orwell distinguishes between the English patriotism that he affirms in the name of the values of the left and the bombastic nationalism that is the cowbird substitute. "By patriotism," he wrote, "I mean devotion to a particular place and a particular way of life, which one believes to be the best in the world but has no wish to force on other people. Patriotism is of its nature defensive, both militarily and culturally. . . . Nationalism, on the other hand, is inseparable from the desire for power." Orwell leaves some difficult questions in abeyance: Can you be patriotic if you don't think the place and the way of life you are devoted to are the best in the world? Can you think some aspects (democracy and human rights) are most definitely worth spreading—even at times by force, come to that, though not cavalierly—and others most definitely are not? I'll come back to these difficulties later, but the important thing is that they complicated the devotional feeling that I had but didn't erase it.

A few days later my wife and I decided to hang an American flag from our terrace. It was a straightforward household decision—hardly a decision at all, because neither of us nor either of my stepsons felt like debating it. There was no controversy and we didn't consult anyone. The flag was a plain affirmation of membership. We did not put it up to claim that the United States of America deserved to rule, or war on, anyone else. (As it happened, we supported the use of force against al Qaeda and the Taliban in Afghanistan, though with plenty of worries about terrible consequences that might ensue, but the worries were neither here nor there.) A few days later Clyde Haberman, a metropolitan columnist of the *New York Times,* called to ask me about the efflorescence of the American flag all over the city. I told him that we had put up a flag, that we had never thought that we would undertake such a display, that it was not meant as support for the policies of George W. Bush but as an affirmation of fellowship with an injured and resolute people. Our private fact was briefly transformed into a news item, featured in Haberman's column of September 19, whereupon a lot of friendly mail came my way, and some not so friendly: some tut-tuts, some insults.

Why this fervent debate? Why did left-wingers of my generation get into arguments with their children, who wanted to fly flags from their windows? Why should many intellectuals have seen the flag as a betrayal? What was it betraying?

For many in the cosmopolitan class, middle to upper middle in income, college educated and beyond, university and culture-industry based, patriotism lost its allure decades ago. This is in large part a story of the "Vietnam generation," but we will also have to look further to comprehend the problem.

To understand why patriotism has been tainted, it will help to consider the opposite concepts against which patriotism is counterposed, for they suggest what people think they are turning toward when they turn away from patriotism. One contrary is individualism, the other, cosmopolitanism.

First of all, patriotism gets in the way of individualism. For patriotism affirms that we are bounded, attached, unfree. It places value on a certain conformity. Nietzsche associated patriotism with the herd instinct. We pride ourselves on being individuals, after all. This is an article of faith, our modern gift, glory, and burden. We are self-created (or trying to be). However and wherever we were born, with whatever roots and equipment, into whatever class, race, religion, region, or nationality, we insist that we remain free to choose the essentials of our lives, that our freedom is inalienable, that whoever tampers with it is our enemy. Choice is our mantra. As women and men with reproductive rights, we declare ourselves pro-choice. As voters, believers, advocates, consumers, we are nothing if not free—or so U.S. intellectuals are inclined to believe, even if, paradoxically, we simultaneously believe that human beings are shaped by society. Even as religious souls, Americans like to imagine that they are born-again, affirming a choice to *accept* Jesus Christ, something they can do or refrain from doing, something that wasn't preordained by the rites to which their parents subjected them.

But patriotism decrees that we are not free. We are obliged. Patriotism is sticky. It is imperious about its imperatives. It values a certain unfreedom, for it declares that in a crucial way we are not free to choose the condition we were born into. Unless we are naturalized citizens, we did not choose our obligation. We are free to imagine our country any way we like, but we are not free to deny that it *is* our country. In fact, patriotism in the United States is an especially compelling and demanding sort of patriotism, because the nation is founded on an idea, not on blood. The idea is an apparent paradox—that we are most ourselves when we affirm our roots, that we are free now because we are bound by the American past. What we are loyal to is the condition of our freedom, and yet when we are loyal, we have renounced our freedom.

All this is to say that if you believe that you are free and that it is important to be free, patriotism, to the degree that it claims your loyalty, is unnerving. The more insistent the claim, the more unnerving it is. One way to ward off the claim is with cosmopolitanism, which by one definition in *The American Heritage Dictionary of the English Language* means a belief that one is "so sophisticated as to be at home in all parts of the world." From a cosmopolitan point of view cosmopolitanism embraces the cosmos, patriotism the parish—it is parochial. The cosmopolitan impulse is to declare that patriotism is for other people—people mired in false consciousness and bad taste, vulnerable to propaganda, bluster, and sentimentality. The nation is what they have—or fancy they have—when they don't have much else.

Cosmopolitanism is not only a belief but an experience. It rests on sociological realities—inexpensive travel, comfort with multiple languages, a thick mesh of contact with people of other nations who affiliate by professional and political interest. The world that cosmopolitans inhabit is not confined to national boundaries. Cosmopolitans also note that, in the argument of the neatly titled book by the political anthropologist Benedict Anderson, *Imagined Communities*, nations are not natural, organic, objective, or anything of that sort but are the inventions—"constructions"—of intellectuals and the stories that they tell about history and culture. (In the more vernacular rendition a nation is an entity possessed of an army, a navy, and a dictionary.) Nations, being constructed, are artificial, not natural, malleable, not fixed. Patriotism therefore loses its primordial aura.

For a large bloc of Americans my age and younger, too young to remember World War II—the generation for whom "the war" meant Vietnam and perhaps always will, to the end of our days—a powerful experience underlay the case against patriotism, as powerful an eruption of our feelings as the experience of patriotism is supposed to be for patriots. Indeed, it could be said that in the course of our political history we lived through a very odd turnabout: the most powerful public emotion in our lives was *rejecting* patriotism.

The United States is a nation that invites anxiety about what it means to belong, because the national boundary is ideological, hence disputable and porous. Part of what it has meant to be American has been to hold views about what it means to be American. As the first constitutional republic the United States has been not just a homeland but a land of ideas, of *Americanism*. When Abraham Lincoln declared, "I have never had a feeling politically that did not spring from the sentiments embodied in the Declaration of Independence,"[1] he was affirming what the radical political theorist John H. Schaar, in a bold essay of 1973, called "covenanted patriotism"[2]—as opposed to the blood-and-soil variety. But under stress the covenant is prone to wear thin. Civic patriotism, which demands self-rule, collapses under the follow-the-leader principle. Under strain authoritarians conclude that questioning authority is an unaffordable luxury. Citizens of the democratic American republic are told that by expounding the wrong ideas, they have forfeited their membership. They are prone, in other words, to be accused of un-Americanism.

Astoundingly, the sixties upended this accusation and turned it into a mass movement of pride. From membership and anger combined came a tradition of antitraditionalism. During most of the sixties, and frequently since, I have groped for words to express, in the right proportions, the membership and the anger at once—the anger deriving from the membership, of course, the membership an intimate fact, making it easy to feel that the nation, by acting contrary to justice, violates its very right to exist. The feeling was: if humanity was betrayed by those who purported to be its saviors, there was no one to rectify the wrong but those of us who understood how deep the betrayal went.

For me the anger predated the Vietnam War. I launched into activism as a campaigner against Washington's nuclear weapons stance in 1960 and only deepened my estrangement from national policies under the pressure of the Bay of Pigs invasion of Cuba, U.S. collusion in South African apartheid, and, deepest of all, the egregious war in Indochina. But for some reason one particular moment in March 1965 stands out. I was twenty-two, living among the SDS circle in Ann Arbor, Michigan, helping organize the first national demonstration against the Vietnam War. The war was already a daily assault on brains and conscience, and so I could scarcely bear to watch the television news. But one evening I turned on the NBC News and saw pictures of U.S. Marines occupying Santo Domingo while young Dominicans protested. It was, on the scale of enormities, only a tiny exercise in old-fashioned imperialism, this expedition into the Caribbean to shore up a military regime blocking the restoration of an elected social-democratic government that it had deposed. There was no napalm, no white phosphorus, no strategic hamlets. I don't know why these particular pictures of young Dominicans resisting the Americans stirred me so deeply, but I know I identified with them. I don't know what I felt more keenly: horrified disbelief that my country could be waving the wrong flag, betraying its better self, or horrified belief that my country could be doing something so appalling only because it—not its policies, not this or that wretched decision, but it in the core of its dark heart—was committed to suppressing the rights of inconvenient peoples. Gunboat diplomacy, we learned to call this, in high school history. How do you reform a leviathan?

I remember writing a poem that night—not a good one but a sincere one. I was a nonviolent twenty-two-year-old and I wanted to stand with the young anti-Americans in the Dominican Republic: the poem ended with a romantic line about "a rifle and a sad song." Another phrase I like better sticks out in my memory: "I would only curse America, like a drunkard his bottle." America, love it and leave it at once. A nice trick, though it may put a kink in your lower back.

I have felt such moments of horrified recognition countless times since and devoted many waking hours to fighting against imperious American foreign and military policies. I am not speaking solely of my ideas here but of passions. In the second half of the sixties and early seventies, I was choking on the Vietnam War. It felt to me that the fight against the war had become my life. The war went on so long and so destructively, it felt like more than the consequence of a wrongheaded policy. My country must have been revealing some deep core of wrongness by going on, and on, with an indefensible horror. I was implicated because the terrible war was wrapped in my flag—or what had been my flag. Then why persist? Why not surrender title, and good riddance? The American flag did not feel like my flag, even though I could recognize—in the abstract—that it made sense for others to wave it in the antiwar cause.

I was a tactician. I could argue—I did argue—against waving the North Vietnamese flag or burning the Stars and Stripes. But the hatred of a bad war, in what was evidently a pattern of bad wars—though none so bad as Vietnam—turned us inside out. It inflamed our hearts. You can hate your country in such a way that the hatred becomes fundamental. A hatred so clear and intense came to feel like a cleansing flame. By the late sixties this is what became of much of the New Left. Those of us who met with Vietnamese and Cuban Communists in those years were always being told that we had to learn to love our people. In my case it was a Communist medical student in Havana who delivered the message in the waning days of 1967. Love our people! How were we supposed to do that, another New Leftist and I argued back, when our people had committed genocide against the Indians, when the national history was enmeshed in slavery, when this experience of historic original sin ran deeper than any class solidarity, when it was what it meant to *be* American? Lessons in patriotism taught by Communists—a definitive New Left experience drawn from the comedy of the late sixties. Well, we would try.

We would go looking for historical lessons, for one thing. Our historians, proudly revisionist, went looking for "history from the bottom up"—heroic sailors during the American Revolution, slaves in revolt, Native American fighters, union organizers, jailed World War I socialists, Wobblies. But the United States of Richard Nixon was not conducive to our invention of *this* tradition. The American flag did not feel any more congenial as Nixon widened the Vietnam War into Laos and Cambodia and connived in the Pinochet coup; or in the eighties, as Reagan embraced the Nicaraguan contras, the Salvadoran and Guatemalan death squads. To put it mildly, my generation of the New Left—a generation that swelled as the war ground on—relinquished any title to patriotism without much sense of loss because it felt to us that the perpetrators of unjust war had run off with the patrium. Economists of the left were busy proving the necessity of imperialism and the military-industry complex; sociologists were busy proving the iron grip of the power elite; philosophers, the accommodationist bias of pragmatism; historians of science and technology, the usurpation of knowledge by corporate and government monoliths.

If intellectual honesty stopped you from papering over the darkness of U.S. history, then what? After such knowledge, what forgiveness? Surely, the nation had congealed into an empire whose logic was unwarranted power. What was the idea of Manifest Destiny, the onward march westward, if not a robust defense of righteous empire? What was the one-time California senator S. I. Hayakawa's brag about the Panama Canal—"we stole it fair and square"—if not a sly recognition of the truth? America was indebted to slavery for much of its prosperity; the United States lorded it over Latin America (and other occasional properties, like the Philippines) to guarantee cheap resources and otherwise line American pockets; American-led corporations (among others) and financial agencies systematically overlooked or, worse, damaged the freedoms of others. Add that the United States, accounting for less than 5 percent of world population, burns about one-quarter of the world's nonrenewable, climate-melting fossil-fuel energy. If all this lording over did not rise to the level of colonialism in the strict sense, and if it could be acknowledged that empires might have some benign consequences, still, U.S. wealth, resource access, military power, and unilateralism qualified as imperial reach.

From the late New Left point of view, then, patriotism meant obscuring the whole grisly truth of the United States. It couldn't help spilling over into what Orwell thought was the harsh, dangerous, and distinct phenomenon of nationalism, with its aggressive edge and its implication of superiority. Scrub up patriotism as you will, and nationalism, as Schaar put it, remained "patriotism's bloody brother."[3] Was Orwell's distinction not, in the end, a distinction without a difference? Didn't his patriotism, while refusing aggressiveness, still insist that the nation he affirmed was "the best in the world"? What if there was more than one feature of the American way of life that you did *not* believe to be "the best in the world"—the national bravado, the overreach of the marketplace. Patriotism might well be the door through which you marched with the rest of the conformists to the beat of the national anthem.

Facing these realities, all the left could do was criticize empire and, on the positive side, unearth and cultivate righteous traditions. The much-mocked "political correctness" of the next academic generations was a consolation prize. We might have lost politics but we won a lot of the textbooks.

The tragedy of the left is that, having achieved an unprecedented victory in helping stop an appalling war, it then proceeded to commit suicide. The left helped force the United States out of Vietnam, where the country had no constructive work to do—either for Vietnam or for itself—but did so at the cost of disconnecting itself from the nation. Most U.S. intellectuals substituted the pleasures of condemnation for the pursuit of improvement. The orthodoxy was that "the system" precluded reform—never mind that the antiwar movement had already demonstrated that reform *was* possible. Human rights, feminism, environmentalism—these worldwide initiatives, American in their inception, flowing not from the American Establishment but from our own American movements, were noises off, not center stage. They were outsider tastes, the stuff of protest, not national features, the real stuff. Thus when, in the nineties, the Clinton administration finally mobilized armed force in behalf of Bosnia and then Kosovo against Milosevic's genocidal Serbia, the hard left only could smell imperial motives, maintaining that democratic, anti-genocidal intentions added up to a paper-thin mask.

In short, if the United States seemed fundamentally trapped in militarist imperialism, its opposition was trapped in the mirror-image opposite. By the seventies the outsider stance had become second nature. Even those who had entered the sixties in diapers came to maturity thinking patriotism a threat or a bad joke. But anti-Americanism was, and remains, a mood and a metaphysics more than a politics. It cannot help but see practical politics as an illusion, entangled as it is and must be with a system fatally flawed by original sin. Viewing the ongoing politics of the Americans as contemptibly shallow and compromised, the demonological attitude naturally rules out patriotic attachment to those very Americans. Marooned (often self-marooned) on university campuses, exiled in left-wing media and other cultural outposts—all told, an archipelago of bitterness—what sealed itself off in the postsixties decades was what Richard Rorty has called "a spectatorial, disgusted, mocking Left rather than a Left which dreams of achieving our country."[4]

From this left-fundamentalist point of view, America was condemned to the attacks of September 11, 2001, by history—a history made in large part by the United States itself. Didn't the United States aid, inflame, and otherwise pump up a host of Islamist fundamentalists—overtly in Afghanistan, to fight the Russians; and effectively (if inadvertently) in Iran, with its long-running alliance with the shah, thereby fueling the Khomeini revolution; and moreover in support of the Saudi ruling family? The ashes of the World Trade Center and the Pentagon were proof that the furies were avenging, chickens were flying home, American detonations were blowing back. A second argument was appended, based on a principle of responsibility sometimes stated in moral, other times in practical, terms: that dissenters should exert leverage where they stand the greatest chance of proving effective. Even if the hands-on perpetrators were al Qaeda operatives, American dissidents could not conceivably influence the Islamists directly; the only possible leverage was on the U.S. government.

Indeed, the United States does not have clean hands. We are living in tragedy, not melodrama. Recognizing the complex chains of cause and effect that produce a catastrophe is defensible, indeed necessary—up to a point. If only history could be restarted at one pivotal juncture or another! That would be excellent. But the past is what it is, and the killers are who they are. Moral responsibility can never be denied the ones who pull the triggers, wield the knives, push the buttons. And now that fanatical Islamists are at work in real time, whatever causes spurred them, the question remains: what should the United States do about thousands of actual and potential present-day killers who set no limits to what and whom they would destroy? The question is stark and unblinkable. When a cause produces effects and the effects are lethal, the effects have to be stopped—the citizens have a right to expect that of their government. To say, as did many who opposed an invasion of Afghanistan, that the terror attacks should be considered crimes, not acts of war, yet without proposing an effective means of punishing and preventing such crimes, is useless—and tantamount to washing one's hands of the matter. But for taking security seriously in the here and now, and thinking about how to defeat the jihadists, the fundamentalist left had little time, little interest, little hard-headed curiosity— as little as the all-or-nothing theology that justified war against any "evildoers" decreed to be such by the forces of good.

So two Manichaeisms squared off. Both were faith based, inclined to be impervious toward evidence, and tilted toward moral absolutism. One proceeded from the premise that U.S. power was always benign, the other from the premise that it was always pernicious. One justified empire—if not necessarily by that name—on the ground that the alternatives were worse; the other saw empire every time the United States wielded power.

But these two polar tendencies are not the only options. There is, at least embryonically, a patriotic left that stands, as Michael Tomasky has put it, "between Cheney and Chomsky."[5] It disputes U.S. policies, strategies, and tactics—vociferously. But it criticizes from the inside out, without discarding the hope, if not of redemption, at least of improvement. It looks to its intellectuals for, among other things, scrutiny of the conflicts among the powers, the chinks in the armor, the embryonic and waning forces, paradoxes of unintended consequences, the sense immured in the nonsense, and vice versa. It believes in security— the nation's physical security as much as its economic security. It does not consider security to be somebody else's business. When it deplores conditions that are deplorable, it makes it plain, in substance and tone, that the critic shares membership with the criticized. It acknowledges—and wrestles with—the dualities of America: the liberty and arrogance twinned, the bullying and tolerance, myopia and energy, standardization and variety, ignorance and inventiveness, the awful dark heart of darkness and the self-reforming zeal. It does not labor under the illusion that the world would be benign but for U.S. power or that capitalism is uniformly the most damaging economic system ever. It lives inside, with an indignation born of family feeling. Its anger is intimate.

Patriotism is almost always affirmed too easily. The ease devalues the real thing and disguises its weakness. The folklore of patriotism lends itself to symbolic displays wherein we show one another how patriotic we are without exerting ourselves. We sing songs, pledge allegiance, wave flags, display lapel pins, mount bumper stickers, attend (or tune in) memorial rites. We think we become patriotic by declaring that we are patriotic. This is activity but of a desiccated sort. It is striking how many of these touchstones we have now—how rituals of devotion are folded into ball games and concerts, how flags adorn the most commonplace of private activities. Their prevalence permits foreign observers to comment on how patriotic the simple-minded Americans are. But such displays are not so straightforwardly proofs of patriotism at all. They are at least equally substitutes. Schaar's stricture is apt here: patriotism "is more than a frame of mind. It is also activity guided by and directed toward the mission established in the founding covenant."[6] Patriotic activity starts with a sense of responsibility but does not discharge it with tributary rites of celebration and memory. Patriotism in this sense, genuine patriotism, is not enacted strictly by being expressed in symbolic fashion. It is with effort and sacrifice, not pride or praise, that citizens honor the democratic covenant.

To put it this way is to erect an exalted standard. Yet to speak of the burdens of patriotism points to something not so flattering about the patriotism that Americans so strenuously claim. Perhaps Americans celebrate patriotism so energetically at least in part because, when we get past the breast beating, our actual patriotic experience is thin on the ground. Perhaps Americans feel the need to tout Americanism and rout un-Americans precisely for this reason—not because we are such good patriots but for the opposite reason. In the United States we are not much for substantial patriotic activity. Ferreting out violations is the lazy person's substitute for a democratic life. If civic patriotism requires activity, not just symbolic display, Americans are not so patriotic after all.

The work of civic engagement is the living out of the democratic commitment to govern ourselves. Actual patriotic experience in a democracy is more demanding—far more so—than the profession of sentiments; it is more easily advertised than lived up to. Democratic patriotism is also far more demanding than signifying loyalty to the regime. In a kingdom the patriot swears loyalty to the monarch. In a totalitarian society the patriot is obedient in a thousand ways—participating in mass rituals, informing on enemies, joining designated organizations, doing whatever the anointed leader requires. But democratic loyalty is something else, stringent in its own way. If the nation to which we adhere is a community of mutual aid, a mesh of social connections, then it takes work, engagement, time. It is likely to take money. It may take life. It is a matter, to borrow a phrase of 1776, of pledging "our lives, our fortunes, and our sacred honor." It may well require that we curb our individual freedoms—the indulgences that normally we count as the highest of values.

In a word, lived patriotism entails sacrifice. The citizen puts aside private affairs in order to build up relationships with other citizens, with whom we come to share unanticipated events, risks, and outcomes. These citizenly relationships are not ones we choose. To the contrary. When we serve on a jury or in Teach for America or ride in the subway, we do not choose our company. The community we partake of—like the whole of society—is a community of people whom we did not choose. (Thus the embarrassment to the individualistic ideal of self-creation.) The crucial difference here is between a community, consisting of people crucially *unlike* ourselves, and a network, or "lifestyle enclave," made up of people *like* ourselves.[7] Many "communities" in the sense commonly overused today—"the business community," "the academic community"—are actually networks, a fact that the term disguises. Cosmopolitanism is also usually lived out as a network extension: it invites connections with people (usually professionals) like ourselves who happen to live in other countries.

Undemocratic societies require sacrifice, too, but unequally. There, what passes as patriotism is obeisance to the ruling elite. Democracy, on the other hand, demands a particular sort of sacrifice: citizenly participation in self-government. This is not the place to explore the difficult questions of where participation must stop and professional management must start. But the important principle is that the domain of popular involvement should be as large "as possible," the question of possibility itself deserving to be a contentious one. At the very least, at the local level the citizens should approve the agenda for governmental action. The result is twofold: not only policy that takes distinct points of view into account but a citizenry that takes pride in its identity as such. When the citizen enters the town meeting, the local assembly, or the jury, disparate qualifications hardly disappear, but they are tempered, counterbalanced by a common commitment to leave no voice unattended.

Decision making aside, democratic life also requires spheres of experience where citizens encounter each other with equal dignity. Put it another way: A democratic culture is one in which no one is exempted from common duties. Commonality and sacrifice are combined. This is the strong side of what has become known as communitarianism, which has also been called civic liberalism. As Mickey Kaus argued in *The End of Equality*, social equality requires bolstering three spheres: the armed forces and national service; public schools; and adult public domains (transportation, health, day care, public financing of elections). The operative word, of course, is *public*. It is in these sectors that the Republic's commonality lives, on the ground, in time and space. In the armed forces life is risked in common. In national service time is jointly invested in benefits that do not accrue to self-interest. When loopholes are closed, class mixing becomes integral to life. Privilege, however useful throughout the rest of life, can't buy you everything. In public schools privilege doesn't buy superior opportunities. In amenities like public transportation, governments provide what private interests would not, and individuals experience themselves as sharing a common condition. If public spheres dwindle, sheer wealth and income grow in importance.[8]

We also need some common sacrifice of our self-indulgences—not to test our Puritan mettle but to prevent ecological breakdown. Having proven averse to eco-efficiency in production, consumption, and transportation, despite our robust achievements in global warming and air and water pollution, we have a particular responsibility to lean less heavily on the earth. Since oil dependency is a considerable factor behind some of the most egregious U.S. foreign policies, true patriotism is fully compatible with, indeed intertwined with, ecological sanity that reduces fossil-fuel guzzling and promotes sustainable sources like solar and wind power. Yet Detroit automakers steadfastly resist hybrid gas-electric cars and increased fuel efficiency, and Washington permits them to get away with their profligacy. Patriots ought to endorse the environmentalist Bill McKibben's suggestion that "gas-sucking SUVs . . . should by all rights come with their own little Saudi flags to fly from the hood."[9]

Overall, egalitarian culture is patriotism's armature. No matter how many commemorations Americans organize, no matter how many pledges we recite and anthems we stand for, the gestures are inessential. At times they build morale—most usefully when the suffering is fresh—but they do not repair or defend the country. For that, the quality of social relations is decisive. And the contrary follows, too: the more hierarchical and less equal the nation becomes, the less patriotic is its life. Not that the culture as a whole should be in the business of enforcing egalitarian norms—the ideal that populism defended and Stalinism made murderous. But there must be zones of social life, important ones, where the same social goods are at stake for everyone and individual distinction does not buy exemption.

The most demanding, of course, is the military—and it is here, where the stakes are highest and the precedents most grievous, that universality is most important. It must not be possible to buy substitutes, as the wealthy on both sides did in the Civil War. Many are the inequalities that are either morally legitimate or politically unbudgeable, but there must be equalities of sacrifice and encounter—not in order to strip the high and mighty of their individuality but purely and simply to treat everyone equally. Financial sacrifice on the part of the privileged is a proof that money cannot buy anything—it may not even be able to buy the most important thing, namely, personal safety. As long as equality prevails in one central zone of life—the most dangerous zone—the inequality of rewards in other zones does not become the be-all and the end-all of existence.

Many liberals demur. For whatever its merits conscription surely grates upon the ideal of self-control—that is precisely one of its purposes. Let's face it: most of us don't like to be told what to do. Moral preachments not only grate, they offend our sense that the only authority worth taking seriously is the authority of our own souls (or senses). Moral preachments about our duty sound to many Americans, left, right, and center, like claxons of a police state. To live our patriotism we would have to pick and choose, to overcome—selectively—some of the automatic revulsion we feel about laying aside some of our freedoms in the name of a higher duty. To be honest, it isn't clear to me how much of my own initiative *I* would gladly surrender for the common good. But "gladly" is not the point.

The principle of universal conscription is not only an abstract tribute to equality—worthy as that would be—but it undermines cavalier warfare. If the citizens asked to support a war are the ones who will have to fight it (or their relatives are), the hypocrisy factor weakens—the fervent endorsement of war in Iraq, for example, by Republican leaders whose children will not serve and who, for that matter, thought the Vietnam War a "noble crusade" (Ronald Reagan's term) though somehow in their own persons somehow never found time for it. The principle that wars must be popular with their soldiers is a good democratic requirement. Let it not be forgotten that Richard Nixon terminated the draft not to end the war—in fact, he continued the war from the air, killing at a pace that exceeded Lyndon Johnson's—but to insulate it from public exposure and dissent.

Other practical difficulties stand in the way of a draft. The principle of universality clashes with the limited need for troops. The military needs high-end recruits: what happens to universality, then? Should the brass be forced to make work for less-qualified conscripts? Should there be a universal draft for national service, with most draftees assigned to nonmilitary duties? Should there be some sort of lottery component? Legitimate questions not to be settled here. But the principle of *some* universal service should be the starting point.

Equal sacrifice of liberty in behalf of conscription ought to dovetail with equal civic opportunity of other sorts. We talk a lot about equality of opportunity, but as a nation we are ill prepared to amplify the principle—to enlarge it to the right to be healthy, to be cared for, to participate in government. As the elections of 2000 and 2004 demonstrated, we are not even terribly serious about guaranteeing the right to vote—and have one's vote counted. In a formula: Lived patriotism requires social equality. It is in the actual relations of citizens, not symbolic displays, that civic patriotism thrives. In these palpable relations no one is elevated. Status does not count, nor wealth, nor poverty. One person, one vote. Absent these ideals in action, patriotism lapses into gestures—Pledges of Allegiance, not the allegiance itself.

But after September 11, 2001, acts of allegiance were precisely what George W. Bush did not inspire. Leave policy questions aside. A unifying logic links many of his public statements on and after September 11. There is the inadvertently comic spectacle of this man, who spent much of *his* September 11 flying around the country as his staff fabricated security threats, soon thereafter appearing on a television commercial urging people to get back on planes and visit Disney World. In July 2002, pooh-poohing the significance of corporate corruption, and therefore the need for political remedies, he resorted to these words: "I believe people have taken a step back and asked, 'What's important in life?' You know, the bottom line and this corporate America stuff, is that important? Or is serving your neighbor, loving your neighbor like you'd like to be loved yourself?"[10] No contradiction here: the mediocre oilman with the triumphal career expressed the logic of a business civilization—consumption *as* citizenship, political withdrawal as a noble act. His not-so-comic equivalent was urging Congress to stick with tax-cut legislation whose benefits would flow disproportionately to the rich who needed it least.

During World War II children collected scrap metal to link their fate to the country they loved. Air raid wardens did their part. So, of course, did soldiers, sailors, and war workers. So did those who accepted their rations without resorting to the black market. Yet in a drastic break from precedent, Bush proposed to cut taxes (especially for the better-off) in wartime, promoting "bombs and caviar," in the words of the *Los Angeles Times*'s Ronald Brownstein, and guaranteeing "bigger federal deficits and a larger national debt," thus shifting the burden onto our children. "With this push to slash taxes during wartime," Brownstein wrote, "Bush broke from 140 years of history under presidents of both parties."[11]

Forget Afghanistan: after September 11, 2001, millions of Americans wanted to enlist in nation building *at home*. They wanted to fight the horror, to take their fate in their hands, to make community palpable. They wanted to rescue, save, rebuild, restore, recover, rise up, go on. From their governments nothing much materialized by way of work for them, for the principal version of patriotism on offer today demands little by way of duty or deliberation, much by way of bravado. What duty might ignite if it were mobilized now, we do not know. How Americans might have responded if their political leadership had invited them to join in a Marshall Plan that would, among other things, contain anti-Americanism and weaken the prospects of jihadist terror, we do not know. How they would have responded if told that it was now a matter of urgent self-defense as well as environmental sanity to free the United States from oil dependency, we do not know. These invitations were not issued. After some days of mutual aid, patriotism dwindled into symbolism. It was inert, unmobilized—at most, potential. In the current state of conspicuous symbolic patriotism, Election Day is all the politics that most citizens can manage, and for most of them that single day is not the culmination of their political activity, it is the sum of their political activity.

Take it as symbolic, then, that September 11, 2001, was, among other things, New York City's primary election day for Democratic mayoral candidates. The primary was the least missed loss of that day. Terrorists smashed up our political life, as well as our economic and personal lives. Our professionals, our public institutions, and our volunteers roared into action. Our police, our fire fighters, our ironworkers, our emergency workers threw themselves into action in a style that deserves to be called noble. A mayor previously unmarked by eloquence responded eloquently. Take it as symbolic that our official politics, and our loss of them, didn't seem to matter much. Politics didn't live. Citizens of the United States did, rising to the occasion, sustaining one another through mutual aid

A few weeks after September 11, my wife and I took the flag down from our terrace. The lived patriotism of mutual aid was in retreat around us and the symbolic substitute felt stale. Leaving the flag up was too easy. Worse: with the passage of weeks, the hardening of U.S. foreign policy and the Democratic cave-in produced a good deal more triumphalism than I could stomach. The living patriotism of the activist passengers of Flight 93 slipped into the background. Deep patriotism, patriotic activity, did not bounce back. Americans were watching more news for a while, even more foreign news, but the needed political debates about means and ends were not happening. Democrats were fearful of looking unpatriotic—in other words, patriotism was functioning as a silencer.

We needed defense, absolutely—lurking in the background was the formidable question as to why we had not had it on September 11, 2001—but what *was* a "war on terror" that was, in effect and in principle, interminable? It would be declared won (as Secretary of Defense Rumsfeld declared soon after the attacks) when and only when Americans *felt* safe. What kind of war was that, whose outcome depended on a popular mood? What did the administration's pre–September 11 obsession, missile defense, and its reckless demolition of such treaties as Kyoto and antiballistic-missile defense have to do with it? Was there not the disconcerting fact that five or six individuals, most of them plutocrats without a legitimate claim to democratic rule, were calling all the important shots? By the time George W. Bush declared war without end against an "axis of evil" (that no other nation on Earth was willing to recognize as such)—indeed, against whomever the president might determine we were at war against, just when he said so—and declared further the unproblematic virtue of preemptive attacks, and made it clear that the United States regarded itself as a one-nation tribunal of "regime change," I felt again the old anger and shame at being attached to a nation—*my* nation—ruled by runaway bullies, indifferent to principle, playing fast and loose with the truth, their lives manifesting supreme loyalty to private (though government-slathered) interests yet quick to lecture dissenters about the merits of patriotism.

As I write, almost all the goodwill tendered to the United States after September 11, 2001, has vanished. U.S. foreign policy arouses contempt and fear almost everywhere. Most of the world has good reason to believe that truculence and arrogance are the hallmarks of Bush's foreign policy—that they are the heart of his foreign policy. Noting how shabby, sloppy, and evasive were Bush's arguments for a U.S.-British war on Saddam Hussein's Iraq, most other nations concluded that Bush seized upon the September 11 attacks as a warrant for pursuing a generally belligerent approach to the world, not least in his confrontation with Saddam Hussein and the disingenuous arguments Bush made for it. Leave aside for the moment the deficiencies of the other powers' approach to Saddam Hussein. Leave aside, too, the virtues of overthrowing his vile regime, and consider the political-psychological fallout of Bush's aggressive war program. With his ferocious logic—"Either you're with us or you're with the terrorists"—Bush isolated the United States but achieved, domestically, a forced marriage. For a while U.S. politics collapsed into his arms. Perhaps inevitably, U.S. politics and public opinion were seized by—panicked into—war fever. Vengeance and aggression fused and overcame niceties of logic and evidence, with which Bush trifled little or not at all. His inner circle deluded itself and deluded the citizens. As the botched invasion of Iraq showed, self-delusion is his inside group's second nature and lying is their third, or the other way round—the exact relation between the two would tax Henry James.

With dispatch and without much care for diplomacy, Bush and his entourage codified their belligerence into a doctrine of preventive war (misleadingly called "preemptive") enshrined in the unilateralist National Security Strategy issued under his name in September 2002. Rhetorically fortified against the "axis of evil," Bush exploited the momentum of counterterrorism to ready war with Iraq. The trauma of the massacres led many Democrats and independents, as well as nearly all Republicans and most of the press, to embrace his policies in the name of the wounded nation. The embrace persisted. Politics ceased. The Patriot Act was rushed through. Civil liberties were abridged with barely a protest. In the shadow of September 11 most Democrats were not only cowed but convinced that they were morally bound to be cowed—though there were noble, cogent dissents from Al Gore, Senator Ted Kennedy, and Senator Robert Byrd.

As the United States hastened toward an indefinite war footing, the Democrats froze. Mainly, during the midterm election campaign of 2002 and the run-up to the Iraq War, leading Democrats ceded foreign and security concerns to Bush and urged voters to focus on economic disgruntlement. Deferring to Bush's claim to be the authentic voice of security, they refused to condemn his weak counterterrorism record before September 11, his spotty record in financing the nuts and bolts of defense afterward, or the injurious consequences of his unilateralism for the multinational cooperation that counterterrorism requires. When Georgia Republicans linked the incumbent Democratic senator and Vietnam War triple amputee Max Cleland with Osama bin Laden and Saddam Hussein in a vile television commercial, the Democrats didn't fight back resoundingly with a how-dare-you. They gave Bush a free hand.

So Bush abused presidential power and rode roughshod over obstacles. To what degree he bewitched himself and to what degree he knowingly bamboozled the public is a nice question.

How much the members of his entourage were lying, how much deceiving themselves, how much cherry-picking the evidence, how much covering up the counterevidence and the complications and the duty of thinking through consequences, how much they were playing the bully's game of triumph of the will—sifting through all the evidence would require a book of its own. But the pattern of blunders and falsehoods is clear. Whatever the proportions that fed their misconduct, they were seized by fantasies of imminent danger and easy occupation, whereupon they lowballed the requisite number of troops, thus bungling the restoration of order in Iraq, ushering in the depredations of looters, and inviting general mayhem. The smug, faith-based ineptitude of the Bush camp recruited more terrorists wordwide and equipped them with new bases in Iraq. By outraging allies, Bush's inner circle squandered trust and endangered the United States. These were the rotten fruits of bad statesmanship.

To put the matter concisely: Bush's White House years put the United States through a time of failing empire and failing democracy both, the big question being, which would fail first? A close question.

Along with some decent outcomes, even the most well meaning of empires bulks up hubris and delusion, which in turn bulk up the machinery of bravado and wishfulness that substitute for reason in a government of runaway power. In the down-to-earth world the dreams of the empire builders rest on fantasy. They must be delusional, because the very real world is recalcitrant. Extraordinary as this may appear to the small minded, people everywhere live in worlds of their own, with their own designs, beliefs, institutions, sins, and prejudices. They will not gladly suffer through occupation even when the occupation overlaps with liberation from tyranny, which in the case of Iraq—don't forget—it did.

George W. Bush's notorious inability to explain himself cogently, as if blunt repetition were an adequate substitute for argument, was more than an idiosyncrasy. It spoke for the miserable standards that prevail throughout a degenerating democracy— but let me hasten to add, a degenerating democracy with a chance of restoring itself to life. The problem was not just that Bush catered to his base of apocalyptic Christians and antitax fanatics but that tens of millions of them were pining for him—and a supine media bent over backward to give him the benefit of the doubt. So did failing democracy go to work for doomed empire.

The point deserves repeating: first in 2000 and then again in 2004, the country had no objection to bullying—that has to be faced. First, almost half of American voters chose this lazy ne'er-do-well, this duty-shirking know-nothing who deceived and hustled his way to power largely without careful scrutiny. It's hardly irrelevant that the Bush pack bulled their way to power partly on the strength of their ignorance. The character of the president is not irrelevant—it takes the measure of our corrupted democracy. His career was nothing if not a protracted exercise in getting away with overreach. The life lesson he learned from broken democracy is that you could drink yourself into one stupor after another, for decades, cover up holes in your c.v., lose piles of other people's money in bad oil investments, and still hustle up more of other people's money for a better investment (in baseball), which you use as a launch to the governorship, then raise piles more money to run for president, and as long as you started with the right genetic stuff, you could come out on top. Then, you and your entourage, including your brother, his staff, and a Supreme Court chosen during your party's long stays in power, stop the Florida recount—and what do you know, you're in power without the nuisance of having to be elected. You could easily feel anointed. A career that culminates in a bloodless coup d'etat gives a man a sense that he can get away with anything he sets his mind to.

What this way of life and governance had to do with democracy was very little. What it had to do with a combination of demagoguery, trickery, and muscle was very much. And so Bush found himself in charge and ready to rip. The words *September 11* were all the argument he needed to fire up for war. The hellish smoke of lower Manhattan would be answered by facts on the ground in Iraq. By the campaign of 2004 Bush had put enough of those facts on the ground to smother doubts about the Iraq War in a conviction that he must be reelected to safeguard the nation against terror attacks that had nothing to do with Iraq. That he accomplished.

Empire in a semi-democracy requires more than the mobilization of fear: it requires delusion about how necessary and easy

empire is. For empire dampens intelligence. It offers recruit-
ment points for the legions who would commit more massacres
out of their own sacred delusions. In the phrase deservedly made
famous by the late senator Daniel Patrick Moynihan, empire "de-
fines deviancy down"—not a charge that the neoconservatives
who used to like it leveled at the Abu Ghraib torturers and their
colleagues at other prisons in Afghanistan and elsewhere. Empire corrupts public debate with demagoguery from every side.

Empire tends to make the winners complacent, belligerent,
stupid, ignorant, and myopic. Harboring the fantasy that the
United States represents only values and not power, empire is
unwilling to face the responsibilities of power, including good
judgment in behalf of those whom empire claims to help.

Empires fade. Inevitably, they grow smug, bite off too much,
inspire too much resentment, collide with too many enemies
too strategically placed. In an age of weapons of mass destruction, where enemies are not strictly of Dick Cheney's or John
Ashcroft's or Alberto Gonzales's invention, the collisions are obviously more dangerous than ever before.

Smugness goes with myopia. For half a century purported
realists in Washington thought nothing of greasing the palms
of Middle East tribal chiefs so that they would grant the favor
of selling their oil. Oil makes the United States grovel before
Saudi tyrants, who funded the Taliban and Wahhabi madrassas
throughout the world. Oil lubricated the disastrous U.S. support
for the brutal shah of Iran—another gift to Islamic fundamental-
ism, as it turned out. Oil floated the tyranny of Saddam Hussein.
Access to Saudi and Gulf oil looks like a triumph of empire but
easily could now be its undoing—not to mention the way the
United States tied itself to Central Asian dictatorships to gain
new oil sources, and underwrote counterguerrilla military action
in Colombia to protect an oil pipeline.

So empire makes the United States myopic and takes its re-
venge on democracy. Ignorance comes to look like innocence—
or, in the current jargon, "optimism." Isn't this the pathos of empire—that, even in the face of murderous attacks, it should go
on protesting its innocence, blinking at an infuriated world, and
protesting that it can bulldoze its way through reality?

During the Bush years intellectuals have had their work cut out for them exposing the arrogance of empire, piercing its rationalizations, identifying its betrayal of patriotic traditions. But all that said, serious questions remained about what intellectuals of the left *wanted*: What *was* to be done about fighting the jihadists and improving democracy's chances? What roles made sense for the United States, the United Nations, NATO, or anyone else? What was required of governments, nongovernmental organizations, foundations, and private initiatives? Given that the Iraq War had been ill advised, what should be done next about Iraq and Iraqis? About such questions many intellectuals of the left were understandably perplexed—and sometimes evasive. Foreign policy wasn't "their problem." Their mode was critical and back-glancing, not constructive and prospective. It was useful to raise questions about the purposes of U.S. bases abroad, for example. It was satisfying, but not especially useful, to think that the questions answered themselves. So the intellectuals' evasion damaged what might have been their contribution to the larger debate that the country needed—and still needs—on its place in the world and how it protects itself.

Liberal patriots would refuse to be satisfied with knee-jerk answers but would join the hard questions as members of a society do—members who criticize in behalf of a community of mutual aid, not marginal scoffers who have painted themselves into a corner. Liberal patriots would not be satisfied to reply to consensus truculence with rejectionist truculence. They would not take pride in their marginality. They would consider what they could do for our natural allies, democrats abroad. They would take it as their obligation to illuminate a transformed world in which al Qaeda and its allies are not misinterpreted as the current reincarnations of the eternal spirit of anti-imperialism. They would retain curiosity and resist that hardening of the categories that is a form of self-protection against the unprecedented.

Even the unprecedented has a history. What happened on September 11, 2001, could have happened only under the appalling spell of a titanic failure of intelligence, or rather, many intersecting failures: the government's failure to know facts; its failure to absorb facts, to "connect the dots"; not least, in the background, a whole society's failure (including the government's but not limited to the government's) to grasp the dynamics of Islamism and defend against its murderous threat.

War was declared on Americans, and in such circumstances "know your enemy" is an imperative not to be neglected. Like any citizen whose knowledge is circumscribed—that is to say, like virtually every American—I wanted guidance in understanding the global Islamist movement and opposing it well. So after September 11, I turned to a range of experts, their scholarship and debates. Even now, I cannot say that my knowledge is deep, but after reading around I feel justified in concluding that, while scholars of Islamism disagree about many things, they agree that it is a force in its own right, not the West's shadow or doppelgänger, not a "construction" of American xenophobes—a force. However deeply, stupidly, self-defeatingly U.S. policy might have inflamed ferocious anti-Western passions in Iran, in Afghanistan, in Egypt, in Saudi Arabia, and elsewhere, still and all, al Qaeda and its allies exist as a world force, a lethal and unremitting movement that a U.S. community of mutual aid must resist—intelligently. And must defeat—definitively. U.S. foreign policy has trampled democratic values and realistic limits along the way, but denouncing these blunders, while probably useful for avoiding repetitions—at least if the hectoring gets through to some of the powerful—is not enough.

Intellectuals must question, certainly. They must question the powers that be—but why stop with the powers? Mustn't we question the counterpowers as well, in hopes of helping them think more clearly? Mustn't we ask of the fundamentalist left, predisposed to think that any American use of force serves imperial interests and that military withdrawal from far-flung bases is automatically the route to safety, whether these assumptions are logical? Are all military deployments equally wrong (or right)? The discussion must be more pragmatic than pointing the finger at evildoers—anti-Americans *or* Americans. Combating global terrorists is a genuine national interest and also a global one but how to combat them *wisely*? Like Paul Berman, who published a polemic, *Terror and Liberalism,* in 2003, I concluded that Islamism, or political Islam, is a poisonous, nihilist, totalitarian creed allied, in its ideological DNA, to fascism and communism. Unlike him, I concluded that its roots are principally non-Western and that the wrong interventions—as against Iraq's Ba'athist tyranny—are likely to backfire.

We are entitled to a sharp debate on the right means of defense, which would hinge, in important part, on understanding the obvious: that all policies have consequences—consequences that need to be hard-headedly assessed. Polemics against evildoers will not do. Neither will neoconservative declarations that all nations that the president designates as members of an axis of evil are equally worth attacking. But the fundamentalist left is almost as empty as the neoconservative belligerents. In the eyes of such figures as Noam Chomsky and the late Edward Said, an American use of force always amounts to one thing and one thing only: the Empire is Striking Back. In their eyes Bill Clinton's interventions in behalf of the rights of Bosnian and Kosovar Muslims were as wicked as any and all other interventions. It follows that there is no interesting divide in U.S. motives or strategies and therefore nothing to choose in U.S. politics. Politically, therefore, the fundamentalist left is not only morally and strategically mistaken, it is hopeless: it cannot possibly outorganize the powers that be, for they are all of a piece. Viewing U.S. power as an indivisible evil, the fundamentalist left has logically foregone the possibility of any effective opposition beforehand.

The fundamentalist left, in other words, is misguided and unhelpful in a distinctive way: it negates politics in favor of theology. It wheels away from the necessary debates about where to go from here. It takes refuge in the margins, displaying its clean hands, and recuses itself. The authoritarians who charge dissenters with treason are paranoid and guilty of bad faith, but the dissenters who concede security to the authoritarians have surrendered the chance of defeating them.

More than three years after September 11, 2001, I'm still within reach of the emotions that welled up then—pain at the losses, fury at the enemies of humanity who hijacked the jets and would cheerfully commit more mass murders, impatience with their apologists. But these reactions are knotted together with anger at the smugness of most of Bush's responses, a passionate revulsion at his reckless foreign policy and in particular his clueless Iraq War, however beneficial some of its consequences.

What follows now for intellectuals? Dissent, for one thing—vigorous, thoughtful, difficult, indispensable. Dissent against the grain, including the grain of the prevailing dissent. Refusing to take conventional wisdom for granted is, after all, the intellectual's calling. The critical spirit at its highest is the same as the scientist's: careful scrutiny of the reigning hypotheses, refusal to bend to authorities or antiauthorities without good reason, skepticism about premises—even the opposition's. But we also need a firm foundation for oppositional politics: a clear vision of values; a convincing analysis of national strengths and failings; a steady, accessible source of ideas about how a country that has lost its bearings can find them. We need, in short, heirs to David Riesman, C. Wright Mills, and Irving Howe.

Patriotism has no quarrel with robust dissent. To the contrary: slack-jawed acquiescence to the authorities, however reverent, however bombastic, is the spirit of defeat—a travesty of patriotic resolve. Patriotism is not obedience. It does not march in lockstep. It is not Ari Fleischer's appalling declaration that Americans should "watch what we say." It is not former attorney general John Ashcroft's admonition: "To those who scare peace-loving people with phantoms of lost liberty, my message is this: Your tactics only aid terrorists for they erode our national unity and diminish our resolve." Obedience is obedience, and there are good times for it—heeding the fire marshals in a crowded theater, for example. But the fact that obedience can be passed off as patriotism in the United States today suggests the poor condition of actual patriotism.

Liberal patriotism would stand a decent chance of rousing dormant political energies—some has already been ignited by George Bush's recklessness and incompetence. Despite the Bush administration's bullying belligerent tactics, most of the U.S.

public still cares about acting abroad through alliances and with the sanction of the United Nations. It is skeptical of go-it-alone adventures. Months of government propaganda, obsequious journalism, and opposition surrender were required to turn public opinion toward unilateral war in Iraq. Not only Democrats but independents and some Republicans ought to find liberal patriotism congenial, though some will bridle at the "liberal" label. On the domestic front little love is now lost for the corporate chiefs, those of gargantuan appetite for whom this administration so loyally fronted until it was shocked—shocked!—to discover there was gambling going on in the casino. With the bursting of the stock market bubble, deregulation à la Enron and cronyism à la Halliburton no longer look like economic cure-alls. Whom do Americans admire now, whom do we trust? Americans did not take much reminding that when skyscrapers were on fire, they needed fire fighters and police officers, not Enron hustlers or Arthur Andersen accountants. Yet we confront an administration that gaily passes out tax largesse to the plutocracy, whose idea of sacrifice is that somebody in a blue collar should perform it for low wages.

Surely, many Americans are primed for a patriotism of action, not pledges or SUVs festooned with American flags. The era that began on September 11, 2001, would be a superb time to crack the jingoists' claim to a monopoly of patriotic virtue. Instead of letting minions of corporate power run away with the flag (while dashing offshore, gobbling oil, and banking their tax credits), intellectuals need to help remake the tools of our public life—our schools, social services, transport, and, not least, security. We need to remember that the exemplary patriots are the members of the emergency community of mutual aid who fought to bring down Flight 93, not the born-again war devotees who cherish martial virtues but were always at pains to get themselves deferred from the armed forces.

Post-Vietnam liberals have an opening now, freed of our sixties flag anxiety and our automatic rejection of the use of force. To live out a democratic pride, not a slavish surrogate, we badly need liberal patriotism, robust and uncowed. For patriotic sentiment, that mysterious (and therefore both necessary and dangerous) attachment to the nation, moves only in one of two directions: backward, toward chauvinistic bluster and popular silence, or forward, to popular energy and democratic renewal. Patriotism, as always, remains to be lived.

It is time for the patriotism of mutual aid, not just symbolic displays, not catechisms or self-congratulation. It is time to diminish the gap between the nation we love and the justice we also love. It is time for the real America to stand up.

Notes

1. Lincoln, quoted in John H. Schaar, "The Case for Patriotism," *American Review* 17 (1973): 70.
2. Schaar, "The Case for Patriotism," p. 68.
3. Ibid., p. 59.
4. Richard Rorty, *Achieving Our Country: Leftist Thought in Twentieth-Century America* (Cambridge, Mass.: Harvard University Press, 1998), p. 35.
5. Michael Tomasky, "Between Cheney and Chomsky," in George Packer, ed., *The Fight Is for Democracy* (New York: HarperCollins, 2003), pp. 21–48.
6. Schaar, "The Case for Patriotism," p. 72.
7. Robert N. Bellah et al., *Habits of the Heart: Individualism and Commitment in American Life* (New York: Harper and Row, 1985), p. 72, uses the term *lifestyle enclave*. The commonplace use of *network* came later.
8. Kaus argued in his 1992 book that liberals are mistaken to overemphasize economic inequality, and I do not follow him all the way to his bitter end. Surely, the appalling inequalities in the ratio between CEO and worker salaries, for example, of the order of 500 to 1, do not serve the entrepreneurial purposes that laissez-faire advocates rejoice in. That it would take confiscatory tax rates to eliminate this discrepancy does not mean that lesser reductions are pointless. Reducing the high-low income gap would work toward the principle of social equality.
9. Bill McKibben, "It's Easy Being Green," *Mother Jones*, July–August 2002, p. 36.

10. Judy Keen, "Bush Trying to Ride Out Corporate Flap," *USA Today,* July 12, 2002, p. 4A.

11. Ronald Brownstein, "Bush Breaks with 140 Years of History in Plan for Wartime Tax Cut," *Los Angeles Times,* January 13, 2003.

Acknowledgments

"David Riesman's Lonely Crowd": Earlier versions appeared as "How Our Crowd Got Lonely," *New York Times Book Review*, January 9, 2000, and as the foreword to the 2001 Yale University Press Nota Bene edition of *The Lonely Crowd*.

"C. Wright Mills, Free Radical": Parts appeared in different form as "C. Wright Mills, Free Radical," *New Labor Forum*, fall 1999; "Critic and Crusader: The Exemplary Passions of C. Wright Mills," *Los Angeles Times Book Review*, May 28, 2000, and the afterword to the reissue of C. Wright Mills, *The Sociological Imagination* (New York: Oxford University Press, 2000).

"Irving Howe's Partition": Appeared in slightly different form in *Raritan: A Quarterly Review*, summer 2003.

"The Postmodernist Mood": Parts appeared in different form as "Hip-Deep in Post-Modernism," *New York Times Book Review*, November 6, 1988; "Postmodernism: Roots and Politics," *Dissent*, winter 1989; and "Phony Gardens with Real Toads in Them," *Tikkun*, March–April 1989.

"The Antipolitical Populism of Cultural Studies": An earlier version appeared in Marjorie Ferguson and Peter Golding, eds., *Cultural Studies in Question* (Newbury Park, Calif.: Sage, 1997).

"The Values of Media, the Values of Citizenship, and the Values of Higher Education" will appear in Robert Calvert, ed., *Political Education and the Modern University*, to be published by Rowman and Littlefield.

"The Intellectuals and the Flag": Some passages are drawn from articles that I published in 2001 and 2002 on www.openDemocracy.net ("The Turning Point," "Moral Seriousness," "Taking It Slowly," "New York Moralia," "Dear Non-American"); "Blaming American First," *Mother Jones,* January–February 2002; and "Liberalism's Patriotic View," *New York Times,* September 5, 2002. Some appear in different form in my book *Letters to a Young Activist* (New York: Basic Books, 2003). Previous versions of the chapter appeared as "Varieties of Patriotic Experience," in both George Packer, ed., *The Fight Is for Democracy* (New York: HarperCollins, 2003), and Thomas Cushman and John Rodden, eds., *George Orwell: Into the Twenty-First Century* (Boulder, Colo.: Paradigm, 2004).

Many thanks to Marshall Berman, David Bromwich, Brian Morton, George Packer, and Barbara Probst Solomon for comments on various chapters; Andrew Delbanco and Elisabeth Lasch-Quinn for reading and criticizing the manuscript; and Liel Leibovitz for helping to find references.

My editor, Peter Dimock, deserves enormous credit for bringing this book into existence. It was his idea in the first place. When I changed courses in midbook, he was willing to ride out the bumps with me. Sometimes he was generous with praise, sometimes he was generous with criticism, and sometimes he was generous with positive ideas. The first and third were usually easier to take than the second, but all three were indispensable.

Laurel Cook is, as always, my loving and beloved muse.

Index